DR NICK CARR

WHAT HAPPENS NOW?

The essential book
for first-time fathers

ACER Press

ACER Press
First published 2012
by ACER Press, an imprint of
Australian Council *for* Educational Research Ltd
19 Prospect Hill Road, Camberwell
Victoria, 3124, Australia

www.acerpress.com.au
sales@acer.edu.au

Edited by Maureen O'Keefe
Cover design, text design and typesetting by ACER Project Publishing
Cover image: © Jade and Bertrand Maitre/flickr/Getty Images
Printed in Australia by BPA Print Group

Cartoons © Andrew Weldon 2012

Thank you to the Grade 1 children at Richmond Primary School and their teacher, Sue
Wilson, for the pictures of 'My Dad'.

National Library of Australia Cataloguing-in-Publication entry:

Author: Carr, Nick.

Title: What happens now? : the essential book for first-time fathers / Dr Nick Carr.

ISBN: 9781742860589 (pbk.)

Subjects: Fatherhood.
               Father and child.
               Fathers.
               Parenting.
               Infants--Care.

Dewey Number: 306.8742

Disclaimer

FOREWORD

There can be something sweetly heroic about a first-time father. Of course he doesn't know this at the time, but there is much he doesn't know. Suddenly he is in the action at the very heart of life and all that matters. Much is at stake. Suddenly he is holding the baby. Her baby. His baby!

As I remember it, becoming a father was actually more joyous than heroic, but I cannot say with confidence that I did it perfectly well or very easily. I did what I thought was best and what I could. It was a long time ago and I have forgotten the details about the exhaustion and the mess, yet strangely the joy of it remains clear and strong in my mind. Memories of that time may be vague but they still awaken intensely happy feelings that seem to inform and strengthen the present day relationship with my fully grown offspring. Fathering goes on and on.

As humans we fail and are failed, yet we also recover and forgive and set things right. There are not many men who can look back on fatherhood without some measure of uncertainty or regret about the way they did it or what they failed to do but if in hindsight there remains a persistent sense of love and joy then we might imagine that things probably went reasonably well under the circumstances. There are always 'circumstances'.

In the midst of stresses, mistakes and difficult times it bodes well for all concerned if there is an underlying delight that persists, even if it is not obvious, and that a father never loses the feeling that this precious new life he holds gently to his heart is a humbling miracle and a great, uplifting beauty. Men are not famous for talking out loud in these terms and when their child is born the joy can be such that words fail them (even though the tears of bliss may be reliable).

But these feelings are important in the business of caring for the infant. They tell of a new father's natural attunement to his baby; a sensitive adoration that will play a huge part in a man instinctively having some idea about what to do when all the many strange and various new parenting moments start to happen. There is a tender confidence that can come into play in a man; a knowing from out of the blue or from somewhere deep inside after a baby is born.

★ ★ ★

When I was a boy, my own father said a mysterious thing to me about the father–child relationship. 'It's a wise man that knows his own father', he said, and I thought he meant that the man we think is our dad may not necessarily be our biological father. This indeed was a perplexing thing to hear from one's father but after he died I realised what he really meant. He had been telling me that many people do not ever fully know or understand their father; indeed a bleak assessment but one with much truth in it. It's amazing how much the relationship with our father may grow and deepen after he has died. Fathering goes on forever.

While it is absolutely vital that a man gets to know and thoroughly acknowledge his children from the day they are born I think it is also essential that children get to really know their father. This begins from day one and the more the two get to know each other the better. Gradually and over time, and at the appropriate time, I believe a father does well to also reveal his story and the truth of his personality to his children. Not just the fine, upstanding respectable man; the figure of authority and knowledge, but the whole man (as much as possible). The real man. The flawed man. That of course is a lifetime's work, and takes a lot of courage.

Dr Nick Carr has written here the sort of book I wish had been available when my first child was born. A little book goes a long way. Not only does he clearly and thoroughly present the most sound advice and practical information about the early phase of first-time fatherhood, but he does it simply and briskly, with good cheer and a nice touch of humour that I dare say echoes much of his own fathering experience. Nick speaks with the reliable knowledge and insight of a gifted medical practitioner but also as a man who has clearly taken enormous delight in a very hands-on approach to the care and fathering of his own baby children. Clearly and comprehensively he tells what needs to be known, yet wisely he allows us to see just enough of who he is as a father and a human being – thus giving a warm heart to the information and underlining the important truth of what a deeply personal, original and organic thing is this strange yet entirely natural business of first-time fatherhood.

Michael Leunig

CONTENTS

ABOUT THE AUTHOR

DR NICK CARR IS a GP in St Kilda and previously associate lecturer in the Department of General Practice at the University of Melbourne. He trained at Cambridge University and Charing Cross Hospital, London before moving to Melbourne in 1988.

Nick has a long-standing interest in parenting, particularly the issues facing first-time fathers. He worked in paediatrics in London and thought he knew quite a lot about how to be a parent until he became one. Twenty-one years and three children later, he now knows a lot more about what he didn't know before.

True to his chosen career as a generalist, Nick has published on a wide range of subjects, from sore throats to computing, baby sleep programs, enemas, sport, psychotherapy, benzodiazepines, consumer issues, personality disorders, fatigue and chicken bones. And parenting.

DEDICATION

To my own parents, who were more than good enough, much more.

To Simon, Isabelle and Olivia, my three wonderful children, who taught me what kids need from their dad.

And to my lovely wife, Sarah, an amazing partner and brilliant mother, who made being a good dad so much more possible.

Becoming a father,
That is no achievement.
Being one is, though.

LES MURRAY,
a Swiss saying from his late mother-in-law Berta Morelli.

INTRODUCTION

THIS BOOK BEGAN WITH an episode of diarrhoea. Charming, I know, but bear with me – it gets better.

I was only four or five years old, and I don't know what upset my tummy, but whatever it was had made a good job of it. I was on the toilet, I was in a mess, and I needed help. I called out to my Mum, she came, and in that wonderfully practical way that mums have, she sorted me out.

Even at that tender age, however, something struck me. Both my parents were at home, but it was Mum's name I called. It hadn't occurred to me to call out for my Dad. 'Dad, come and help clean me up'? Unthinkable. I loved my Dad, he was great, and not one of those pipe-and-slipper fathers who I only saw to kiss goodnight at bedtime. But even if he had been the only parent in the house, there's no way I would have asked him to come and wipe my bum.

As I grew older, something about this story stuck in my mind. I thought about the kind of father I would like to be if I were ever lucky enough to have children. (Don't get me wrong, I wasn't completely weird. I also did normal teenage things like kick balls, fail to tidy my room and have some of those magazines hidden under my mattress.) I always had this sense that – please excuse the double negative – I did not want to be the kind of dad who couldn't help when his child was in a mess.

Then I was lucky enough to meet a wonderful woman and I became a first-time father. Time to get serious and do some research. I talked to a lot of people, read everything I could find, and was immeasurably helped by the fact that my wife was herself very smart in this whole parenting territory. What I wanted to know about was the concept of what might be called the 'nurturing' father. Was it possible for a dad to have a more significant role in the caring and nurturing of his child? And if so, what might be the barriers, and what might help? I also wanted to try to understand why so many first-time fathers were asking the same question: 'What happens now?'

One of the first things I discovered, to my relief, was that the concept of the nurturing father has in fact been well researched. By observing fathers caring for their babies, and measuring all sorts of details such as responsiveness to infant cues and eye contact and so on, the researchers found that fathers were just as capable as mothers of providing effective, nurturing care. Phew, I thought, at least I'm not completely wasting my time. Hurdle one successfully cleared.

The next question was: 'Does it matter?' I mean, nice idea and all that, being more involved with my children, but apart from a warm fuzzy glow, was it going to make any difference? Again, the answer seemed to be a resounding 'yes'. It's not easy research to do, but the experts have concluded that having a caring, involved father has some major potential benefits for infants and children as they grow older. Better educational outcomes, better psychological health, less police contact, and better marital relationships were all found to be associated with involved fathering. This was true for both sons and daughters, but particularly for sons. Oh, and the children have better relationships with their fathers. Several more hurdles seemed to have been cleared.

Then it started to get interesting. If being an involved father (a) works and (b) makes a real difference to all concerned, why hadn't it been standard practice since, well, since forever? Why had previous generations of dads seemed so distant from their kids? If it was hard for new dads to get involved, what might help?

Because of these questions, I have spent the last 25 years reading, writing and talking about fathering. I have had the great privilege as a GP to hear first-hand experiences of families, about what works and what doesn't. And I have had three children of my own who have taught me more about how to be a father than everything else put together.

This book is for all you new dads who would like to be closely involved with your family. It is for all you dads who want a strong, meaningful attachment with your new child, and who want to know 'What happens now?' This book is for all of you who like the idea of being able to help your little one in their moment of diarrhoea-est need (sorry, couldn't resist it).

This book is for the kind of father who will feel a warm inner glow when the cry comes from the bathroom, 'Daaaad, I need help!'

CHAPTER 1

THE NURTURING FATHER – WHY IS IT SO HARD?

IS IT HARD? Is getting in there and being properly involved with your child really so difficult? Well, yes and no. There are, I believe, a few obstacles, some more obvious than others. If you just want to get some thoughts about how to be a great dad, skip this bit and head straight for Chapter 2. If you want to understand a bit more about why it can be complicated, and perhaps why it wasn't how your own father did things, read on …

HISTORY

Go back 150 years, only a few generations ago, and Victorian society accepted the idea of the aloof, distant father. Children were to be seen, not heard, and if they could be heard when not invited to be so, it was father's job to exact the punishment. And dad was encouraged to not spare the rod, for fear of spoiling the child. Not exactly our modern idea of the nurturing father.

It goes back a long way. In fact, if we go back a very long way, pre-industrialisation, to our original hunter–gatherer societies, dad certainly didn't spend much time at home then. His job was out and about, away from the cave or the hut or whatever, collecting the food. Picking berries, harvesting nuts, clubbing small furry animals – that sort of thing. Probably not a lot of time spent at home nurturing. In these more ancient societies, the link between sex and reproduction was not even known. Yes, they had sex all right, but nobody had quite twigged that this was what led to the arrival of a baby many phases of the moon later. The mysterious process by which a woman's belly slowly expanded with new life was unknown and considered to be all her own work, clever thing that she was. Perhaps it's not so surprising then that the man was not expected to have much involvement in the caring and nurturing of the outcome.

BLOODY HELL, WHERE DID THAT COME FROM? NOTHING TO DO WITH ME …
MR IVAC LUB, C. 12 000 BC

Industrialisation brought a more distinct separation between work and home, but still it was largely dad's job to go out and earn the money, and mum's job to look after the kids. This continued right through to the Victorian era and beyond – which brings us, almost, to the present day.

How was that for a gross over-simplification of many thousands of years of social anthropology?

No doubt that over the ages countless men adored their kids and wanted to care for them; perhaps some did. But it wasn't what was expected. We talk about it now, at least in Westernised societies, as if it's a standard choice, but it helps to remember that, in terms of the human race, this is a brand-new concept.

PSYCHOLOGY

At the end of the 19th century along came Freud. The big daddy of psychology, you'd think maybe he was the one to recognise the potential of fathers in nurturing their children. Well, Freud was certainly one of the first to consider the mother–father pair as a unit, and the role of both parents in helping the child grow and separate from them to become an individual. But the kind, caring father? Not really. The Freudian father was as likely to chop your balls off as read you a bedtime story (see below).

LOVE YOU, MUM

One of Freud's central theories was that of the Oedipus complex. Everyone knows this as the 'yuck' theory, the one about wanting to have sex with your own mother. Less well-known is that a critical part of the Oedipus theory is the fear of castration. To try and translate an aspect of a complex and ground-breaking theory into simple English, Freud made the following suggestions:

The young son competes with his father for affection from his mother. He observes that his mother/sisters have no penis, and assumes that they have been castrated. The boy believes that his father castrated them, and fears that he will be castrated himself. This understanding and fear help begin his separation from his mother.

Again, hardly qualifies as a description of the nurturing father, does it?

Through most of the 20th century, other experts writing about parenting tended to focus on *mothers* and infants. Fathers remained peripheral. In 1951, a chap called John Bowlby wrote:

> *Nevertheless ... fathers have their uses even in infancy. Not only do they provide for their wives to enable them to devote themselves unrestrictedly to the care of the infant and toddler, but, by providing love and companionship, they support her emotionally and ... In what follows ... little will be said of the father-child relation; his value as the economic and emotional support of the mother will be assumed.*[1]

Bowlby was one of the seriously influential figures in child development. He was a British psychoanalyst and adviser to the World Health Organisation on matters of mental health. He was a champion of the idea that babies and young children need a consistent attachment figure, a theory that remains strongly supported today. But for Bowlby in 1953, women were the important caregivers. Not much of a role for a nurturing father there.

Margaret Mead, a social anthropologist writing in the 1940s, was another who expressed uncertainty about fathers' role. In a chapter titled 'Human fatherhood is a social invention' she wrote:

> ... that men have to learn to want to provide for others, and this behaviour, being learned, is fragile and can disappear rather easily...[2]

Only in the last few decades has psychology really focused on the caring role that fathers can have. So, even for the 'experts' this is relatively new territory.

BIOLOGY

Why is it that, when it comes to biology, we men always seem faintly ridiculous? Women have this nice soft roundedness, all the complicated organs tucked neatly away inside. We have these ungainly bits hanging around the outside, whose aesthetic appeal is appropriately confined to crude depictions on cubicle walls. In one of our medical school shows the ancient caretaker was named Old Scrotum, The Wrinkled Retainer. How apt.

Even a woman's eggs, the ova, are nice, round, sensible little things. Like elegant princesses seeking freedom, they pop out of their ovary tower and sit quietly in the Fallopian tube, awaiting a knight in shining armour. The knights? Millions of ludicrous little sperms thrashing around, each with a windmill tail like some hyperactive terrier.

When one knight succeeds in his quest, a process begins for which modern teenagers have robbed us of a meaningful description. Because what happens next really is awesome. Like, *totally* awesome.

Having a person grow inside you, to feel that person move and kick, to have that complete, physical connection day and night for nine months. How awesome is that? No wonder the physical umbilical cord becomes such a strong metaphorical one, long after its real-world counterpart has been severed. And for mums who breastfeed, the physical connection continues.

And for us men? We walk beside her, her expanding tummy announcing to the world her imminent parenthood. No part of our anatomy expands, inviting strangers to come and touch us, inducting us into this new world. We are separate.

In the old days, we were banned from the delivery suite. Our first sight of our newborn was nicely cleaned and wrapped, peacefully asleep. These days a scrunched-up, blood-stained and screaming creature is laid on our partner's chest, her own screams still ringing in our ears. And that's when it's all gone well.

It doesn't seem to me that biology really does its bit to help dads get in there and feel connected ...

HE'S SO SMALL. HE WAS BORN PREM, I'M SCARED TO HOLD HIM. WHAT IF I DON'T SUPPORT HIS HEAD PROPERLY AND SOMETHING HAPPENS?

IT WAS A 40-HOUR LABOUR. WHEN SHE WAS BORN THEY PUT HER STRAIGHT UNDER THE 'LIGHTS' AND I WENT HOME. THE HOUSE WAS EMPTY AND I FELT SO ALONE, SO, WELL, DEPRESSED ...

SOCIETY

Here in Victoria we used to have Infant Welfare Centres. Then some bright spark changed the name – to Maternal and Child Health Centres. Not much place for a dad there.

It may sound like a small point, but language is important. You will hear people saying about a dad, 'He's babysitting the kids today'. Generally when a mum is with her kids no one says she's babysitting. In fact, no 'verb' is needed. What's she doing today? She's at home with the kids. But what is she actually doing? Parenting? Living? There isn't really an answer, is there? She's just doing what she does. But no-one would say she's babysitting.

When I took my firstborn to the Maternal and Child Health nurse, I asked her about her title, and why it had been changed to specifically exclude me. She looked at me as if I was an alien species, the clear implication being that the title was spot-on.

A major Canadian paper, the *Early Years* study, 207 pages of fascinating bedtime reading, mentions mothers 104 times, but fathers just nine.[3] Are we really only 8.65 per cent as important?

Paternity leave? Never heard of until recent years. I'm not sure the term even existed last century.

One otherwise excellent article on fathering has this in the executive summary: 'While there is increased pressure and expectations for men to become less *gendered* and contribute more to families...'[4] (my italics). Wow, is that what it takes? Turn the masculinometer down? Ease up on the testosterone implants? Thank goodness I was too busy being a (very manly) parent to read that sentence until the kids were older, or I'd have been straight down to my doctor's for a gender reduction.

As for role models, since this whole nurturing dad bit is new, there are few of us who had fathers who showed us how it could be done. 'My dad worked hard, 10, 12 hours a day, to provide for us. I hardly ever saw him' is a common refrain. It's not that we're ungrateful, but it is yet another example why doing it differently is a challenge.

GIVE UP NOW?

All this is a rather longwinded way of saying that, while I strongly believe that being a nurturing father has wonderful rewards all round, there are multiple reasons it's not easy. The result, for a lot of first-time dads, is that it *is* too hard, and they go back to doing it the way it's been done before, the way it has 'always' been done, perhaps to the way it was done to them. Nothing wrong with that; generations of kids have survived quite nicely, thank you, myself and possibly yourself included.

But if you're up for the challenge of doing it differently, read on.

CHAPTER 2
WOW! PREGNANCY

'Darling, I've got something to tell you — I think I'm pregnant!'

'Really? Are you sure?'

'No, I mean I haven't been to the doctor yet, so I'm not really sure. But my period's late, I've done two home tests, both of which were positive, my breasts feel like watermelons and at today's board meeting I brought up the Twisties I had for breakfast. So I think I might be …'

'Wow!'

For some of us, this conversation is a dream come true, for others the reaction may be a bit more mixed. But since this is a book for fathers, let's assume that your first response is *not* acquiring a false passport and taking the next plane to Buenos Aires. What happens now?

That is exactly the question a friend asked me after his first child was born. I popped into his shop to congratulate him.* Everything had gone well and the baby had come home the day before. Felicitations having been offered and accepted, he suddenly looked rather serious and asked, 'What happens now?' It was a genuine question. There's a new, vulnerable little person at home – help!

I had heard this before, this uncertainty from a new dad. It is, I believe, entirely understandable, and goes back right to the start of the process.

For women, there is a whole system around pregnancy that swings into action pretty much straight away. This system sweeps them along, while we men are sometimes left on the sidelines, watching and feeling a tad inconsequential. When a pregnant woman asks 'What happens now?', there is often a barrage of advice from friends, relatives, midwives, doctors, antenatal classes and books to answer the question. From my experience, men also want to know what happens now, but are unsure who to ask. When men do ask, there's a good chance that all they get is a sympathetic shrug, or

---

* Though what, exactly, are we congratulating him for? Holding her hand really tightly while she screamed? Not fainting? Driving mother and baby safely home from the hospital? I'm being facetious, of course – we're celebrating the miracle of birth, the successful result of DNA's longing for itself, to paraphrase Khalil Gibran. That's got to be worth a congratulations.

otherwise something really helpful like a slap on the back and 'Well, that's your fun and games over, mate!'

What actually happens during pregnancy is that all sorts of things happen to and for *her*. She has appointments with doctors, for scans, blood tests; she has long phone conversations with friends about mysterious things like Leboyer, listeria, and pelvic floors; she has people constantly inquiring about how she is. There is often lengthy consideration about the type of birth, pain control methods, natural versus medical delivery and so on. Antenatal classes dwell on birthing options, breathing techniques, the pelvic floor (again …)

These are all important considerations, but it can leave us men wondering what our role is. Indeed, sometimes the emphasis during pregnancy is so strongly about the birth, that the birth itself seems to be the endpoint. It's as if once the baby is born, the rest, whatever that may be, is straightforward. One small fact tends to get sidelined – that after the birth you usually have a child (or even children), and the birth itself soon pales into insignificance compared to the realities of parenting. Many women are shocked to find that, despite diligent attendance at every antenatal class, avid reading of multiple pregnancy books and hours spent scouring 'Mom's room' internet sites, they still find themselves desperately underprepared for the task of being a parent. If this is true for her, it is doubly so for him.

EXCLUSION

What all this adds up to is that pregnancy can be quite excluding for men. Funnily enough, this can still be true despite all the emphasis on the involvement of dads these days. For example, antenatal classes may be held during the daytime, making it harder for the working dad to be there. If we do manage to get there, we find ourselves squatting stiff-legged on leaky bean bags trying to understand the intricacies of epidurals, learning how to pant when instructed and how to rub her back between contractions. Some of us feel empowered and involved, but just as many feel a sense of uneasy irrelevance as we struggle to find our place in this oestrogenic odyssey.

Many men are not all that used to feeling marginalised, peripheral, our needs and preferences secondary to someone else's. So it can be disconcerting to suddenly be in that position at a time when we may have expected to feel central and involved.

So you *may* find yourself feeling a bit excluded. It's important to understand that this is not an uncommon experience for men, and also that this is not *her* fault.

So what is our role in this early stage during pregnancy?

Our role is to be there. What I mean is to be there for her. This stage, pregnancy and planning for delivery, is women's business (without the secrets) and what we can do is be there to help, hold, support and listen. And while we're doing all that helping, holding, supporting and listening, we need to keep a bit of an eye on ourselves, just to see how we're travelling. If we start feeling a bit left out, a touch of resentment creeping in, if we start wondering why so much has changed and was this really a good idea, it may be time for a self-check. A bit of internal dialogue perhaps:

'Gee I'm getting pissed off – all I seem to hear about all day is baby this, scan result that, about morning sickness and thrush and pains and discharges and why-can't-you-get-time-off-to-come-to-the-next-antenatal-appointment-to-learn-about-Caesarean-sections. God, anyone would think that ... Hold on a minute, I'm getting to sound pretty crabby, to feel resentful and a bit excluded. I remember reading about that, and how men can end up feeling this way and that sometimes that's just the way it is. I guess I just have to keep that in mind and remember that this is essentially her time, and that my job is – what did it say? – oh yes, just to be there. Doesn't sound like much of a job, but I suppose it's only for a few months. I wonder if there's a beer in the fridge?'

Here's a revolutionary concept – you could even try talking to her about it! But be gentle; she's got a lot on her mind already and doesn't need to feel that she has to look after you as well. By all means chew it over with her, but take responsibility for how you feel and make sure you don't leave her feeling guilty. She needs to know that, despite you feeling a bit out of sorts, you're still managing and are still there for her.

And although nine months sometimes seems like nine years, actually it doesn't take that long. Ask anyone who's got a five-year-old and they'll put the whole pregnancy thing in perspective for you: 'Oh that – yeah, I think I remember ...'

So hang in there.

CHAPTER 3

VENUS AND MARS

Something has happened – a fight with a friend, another disagreement with her mother, her sister's moved in with the unsuitable boyfriend. What's her first response? Ring up someone and talk about it – at length, dissecting every detail, reworking every utterance, interpreting and reinterpreting. And then? Ring up someone else and have the same conversation all over again. We men sit there alternately bemused and frustrated – bemused because it makes no sense to us at all, frustrated because it seems such a pointless waste of time.

As astronomers debate the possibility of life millions of light years away from our own solar system, researchers here on earth have finally proved what most even semi-conscious people have known for generations – men and women think differently. When something is on *her* mind, her approach is usually to talk about it, apparently endlessly, including – shock horror – talking about how she feels. When *we've* got a problem, we tend to respond by looking for solutions, trying to work out how we can fix it. This is fine with a squeaky door hinge on a fridge (oil) or feeling frustrated with work (open noiseless fridge, extract beer, watch footy), but unfortunately doesn't work quite as well when we apply our solutions to her concerns.

For example, when my wife was pregnant for the first time, she was very anxious about whether the baby was OK. Blood tests and scans were fine, but she was still anxious, so I suggested further tests. They were OK too, but she was still anxious. I started becoming irritated, getting all blokey and logical: 'We've done all these tests, they're all normal, why are you still worried? What else do we have to do?' Here of course is the clue – I was so busy trying to work out what to do, how to 'fix' the problem, addressing the problem in my rather pathetically inappropriate masculine way, that I'd completely missed the point. She kept telling me I wasn't helping, and eventually I managed to bleat, 'I don't know what else to do', which prompted my wife to cotton on to what was happening. This, more or less, is what she said:

'You don't have to fix anything! There's nothing very logical about my anxiety, nothing that any number of tests or other practical stuff is going to make much difference to. It's just that this is my first pregnancy, it's strange and scary and wonderful and there's a lot that I don't really

understand and I've wanted this so much and I'm frightened of all the things that could go wrong. I know all the scans and so on are fine but I still can't help feeling worried and I wake up at night just wondering and nothing anyone can do or say will stop me worrying...'

(Me: frustrated, confused, failing to hide my anger) *'So if nothing will stop it, what do you want me to do?'*

'I want you to stop offering advice and suggestions about how to sort it out and I need you not to get annoyed with me. I need you just to listen, to give me a hug, let me cry without feeling you have to offer a solution. I need just to be able to say I'm worried and know that you're still here to be with me, that you can listen without getting cross. You don't really need to say anything much, just make me a cup of tea and give me a long cuddle.'

This was something of a revelation; don't say much, make tea, give cuddle – hey, I can do that! It made me realise how unhelpful my previous approach had been. I had completely failed to understand her perspective. I had embarked on a series of complex and useless attempts to 'fix' things when, paradoxically, what I was actually being asked to do was incredibly simple. I just hadn't known.

Men are straightforward creatures. Give us an instruction book and we can assemble an IKEA wardrobe, give us a recipe and we can cook. (But what the hell is Sambal Oelek?). However, my wife didn't come with a manual, and I was too dumb to ask for a step-by-step guide. When she finally did tell me what to do it was such a relief for both of us, and it turned out to be so easy. Boy did I get good at the shut-up–tea–cuddle bit! Tears flowed, tissue boxes were depleted and I became master of the soothing grunt, the occasional 'It'll be OK' – and we both felt so much better. Her anxiety waxed and waned but was more contained, while I lost most of my frustration and knew better what to do with the bits that remained.

The point of all this? Well, some men are lucky and have already found this out; they've read the right books or are naturally more intuitive or have talked to the right people. But for many, like myself, it is the new and complex emotional time of pregnancy that really brings this communication issue to the fore.

So, a word of advice. If you find yourself getting irritated or frustrated in the sort of way I did, try the shut-up–tea–cuddle approach. Better still, talk to her. Ask what *she* would find helpful, how she would like you to help her. Stop trying to do things in your own practical but essentially masculine way and get her to 'read' to you from her own instruction manual. Like the wardrobe, if you follow the instructions properly, you should find it works well and, unlike the wardrobe, you may be pleasantly surprised to find how easy it is.

CHAPTER 4

THE DELIVERY – SWEET ...

Our babies were born with every high-tech assistance known to the human race: hospital, surgeon, anaesthetist, paediatrician, any number of machines that go ping. Because of this – some cynics might say despite – they arrived safely in the world. When I asked my wife what she remembered most about the experience, she said that with all her fear and anxiety, someone had kept his firm, kind hands on her shoulders, and that she felt very comforted by this. They belonged to the theatre orderly, the guy who'd wheeled her in on the trolley. Surrounded by all the incredible sophistication of modern medicine, her strongest memory was of human touch.

What do I remember of the first time? A sense of separateness, of feeling slightly awkward and irrelevant as the system swirled around me. A system of which I had been a part in the past, but was now outside. I sat where I was told to, holding her hand (a bit too tightly). A vertical blue sheet had been erected halfway down as a visual barrier, metaphorically dividing her body. I tried to concentrate on the drip stand, or the anaesthetist's stubble, anything to avoid thinking in too much detail about the scalpel and the very real divide that was going on south of that blue sheet. I had been on the south side for many Caesarean sections in the past, I knew the process well, but this was my wife. Hold, squeeze, drip stand, concentrate.

And suddenly there he was, our buttery baby, all pink and bloody and uttering only the slightest protest at his sudden emergence into the blaring cacophony of life. A quick check by the paed – healthy – a wipe and a wrap and there he was in our arms. The feeling? Wonderment that it had all worked, and overwhelmingly a sense of relief that he was OK. Connection, a bond, would come later, and with it profound love. For the moment there were other priorities.

Photographs.

HOW MUCH INVOLVEMENT?

Not too long ago the task of the first-time dad was to make sure the wife (rarely 'partner' in those days) was safely under the care of someone else, then go back to work (or down the pub) and wait for news of junior's arrival. Once the call came there were cheers all round, drinks bought and cigars lit – job done.

Fast forward a few decades in time (and light years in expectations) to today. I can't think of too many first-time mums who'd be happy with the work–pub–cigar scenario, but what about the dads? Here we are again in new territory. Despite being a doctor himself, and me being a home birth (my parents weren't hippies – home birth was common in the UK in the 1950s. Yes, I'm that old), my own father was not down the business end helping ease me into the dusty bedroom atmosphere. He wasn't even on hot water and towels duty. He was at work in the outpatients department and no-one, including my mother, expected anything else (though she wishes he had been there). Yet, just a generation or two later, a lot of new dads expect, and are expected to have, greater involvement in labour and delivery.

Pause for a moment and just check. How do you want to do this? How does *she* want you to do it? In Australia, over 95 per cent of babies are born in a hospital. How do you imagine you might feel surrounded by a sterile clinical environment? Are you one of those people for whom steel trolleys or the smell of antiseptic triggers some deep-rooted childhood response, resulting in you swooning into an inelegant, crumpled heap? Or are you one of those for whom the sight of blood and the sound of primeval screaming girds you into action? Wherever you fit on the spectrum, have an honest conversation with your partner about it ahead of time. There are a few points you might want to consider.

CAESAREAN SECTION

Nearly one-third of Australian babies are currently born by Caesarean section. Leaving aside the complex arguments about why this figure is so lamentably high, that still leaves most babies being born vaginally. The options for fathers vary a bit between these two forms of delivery.

Caesarean section is performed in a formal operating theatre, and there are more clearly defined 'rules' about who can do what and where. If she has a general anaesthetic, which is more likely when it's an unexpected or emergency caesar, you won't be invited in. If she has a spinal anaesthetic, which is more common for elective caesars and means she will be awake during the procedure, dads are generally welcome. You will be sat up the top end, where your presence can be enormously important for her.

Operating theatres can be intimidating, and can have funny effects on people. Fainting is common, and doesn't discriminate between the weeds and the rugby players (I was one of the latter, but also an accomplished fainter as a medical student). If you start feeling uncomfortable, tell someone. If you get all woozy, put your head down between your knees. Don't just try and tough it out, as the likely result is you crashing to the floor, taking out the anaesthetist's kneecap on the way down.

VAGINAL DELIVERY

With vaginal births, fathers tend to have more options about what they can do, and often a lot more time to do it. I think we can safely assume that if you've chosen to be there, you're not going to sit in the corner doing the crossword or watching a movie on your smart phone. You may have the option to do things like cut the cord, or you might stick with supporting her as best you can. But be aware that even this can be distressing at times. A partner in pain, sweaty and tired from hours of labour, might be a challenging experience for some men. Are you ready for this?

It's important to decide in advance whether you are comfortable having anything to do with the delivery itself. Even if you are, is your partner? Childbirth might be a miracle, but the process is accompanied by some blunt realities. A vulva swollen and distorted by a baby's head is a sight not easily forgotten. There may be blood. With all that pushing, there may be faeces. If you are the kind of bloke who feels queasy after reading those last three sentences, you may be better off leaving that end to the professionals.

VENUS AND MARS REVISITED

Remember how they (women) are really good at the feeling/thinking side of things, whereas we (men) tend to excel more at the practical/doing? Well, delivery is a funny old reversal of this. She has some seriously practical things to do: push, breathe, push harder, pant, don't push! You have to try to work out how to help her by 'feeling' her emotions and providing support. Thinking ahead is a smart move, as there are a few dos and don'ts.

> Do stick with positive and supportive phrases, such as, 'That's great', 'Well done', 'You're amazing'. 'I love you' is usually acceptable.

> Don't be too instructive. Unless the midwife asks you to, don't tell her when to push or how to breathe. If you're not sure what to do, ask her what would help.

> Do remember that this is all new for her too. There are a zillion hormones doing things to her that she doesn't understand

either. She might say and do things that seem out of character. Roll with it.

> Don't be critical or say something like, 'Whoa, that is so totally not you!' Whatever else you might say, never tell her to 'Just relax'. Ever.

> Do focus on her and her needs. Your main job is just to be there for her. But be prepared to actively advocate for her, if you know there's something she'd want done differently but is not able to make this clear herself.

> Don't plague her with your own anxieties or needs – sorry, these have to wait.

> When the baby is born, do say something positive: 'he looks wonderful' or similar. This is not a time for your quirky humour. 'Aargh, he looks like that squid thing in *Alien*' or 'They were right about babies and Winston Churchill' are not funny. And the staff have heard them all before.

If all goes well, your baby will stay with you, and your partner may be able to try to give him a feed soon after birth. Sometimes your baby may need some medical attention, or may need to go into an incubator to warm up. The latter happened with our firstborn. I was asked whether I wanted to go with him, or stay with my wife. I stayed with her. I have no recollection of this little vignette, but 20 years later my wife surprised me by telling me that it was one of the most important things I'd done. Given the choice between our new baby and her, I'd stayed with her. Which was, apparently, exactly what she'd needed. I'd got it right!

I could so easily have got it wrong. But it makes sense, doesn't it? Your baby will only go somewhere else because something needs to be done, and there will be people there to look after him. He can manage without you, but for now it's your partner who really needs you there. So don't do what I did and leave it to chance. Plan ahead. If you're given the same option, unless your partner makes it clear she wants to be left alone, I suggest you say in a strong, firm voice, 'Thank you, but I'm sure you'll take good care of our baby. I'll stay here with Vashni/Veronica/Waleria (delete as appropriate) – my place is with her'. Minimum 20 years' appreciation assured.

VIDEO

Don't. You're starting a family, not making a documentary. You're there to participate, not to be an observer. You're there to hold her hand, to comfort and encourage, not to shove a camera lens up her nose and ask her to smile as she tries to push something akin to a small rockmelon through her cervix.

And anyway, has anyone ever watched them subsequently?

Photos are different. Take plenty, but take them later, when all the, ahem, push and shove is over. You'll need them for his 21st.

THE PENDULUM

I mentioned at the start that the swing towards encouraging dads to be at the birth is relatively new. It's been a strong swing, and it is now assumed that most dads will be there and that this is a Good Thing. But it's worth knowing that there are dissenting voices. Only a few years ago, a senior British obstetrician went public with his view that men in the delivery suite gain little benefit for themselves or their partners.[5]

I'm always suspicious of pendulums. When they swing rapidly and determinedly in one direction, you can pretty much guarantee a correction at some point. How strong that correction will be only time and the retrospectoscope can tell us.

So, why do I mention this? Well, there may be some new dads out there who, for whatever reason, feel uncomfortable about being present for the birth of their child. I don't want those men to feel forced into a decision because of the pendulum effect. Personally, I believe that we should encourage men to be involved, but that doesn't mean either that I'm right or that it's right for you. If you're not sure, get informed and talk to people about it. Most importantly, have an honest conversation with your partner.

MORE INFORMATION

Not surprisingly, labour and delivery is a huge topic, and there is a large amount of information out there. There are plenty of excellent sites that provide facts and advice. One Australian site (sponsored by Johnson's® baby, but full of good content) is <www.babycenter.com.au>. A good alternative, written by a midwife, is <www.pregnancy.com.au>. Both of these sites have good information and links relevant to dads. For dads specifically, the choice in Australia is more limited. Try <www.imgoingtobeadad.com.au>.

CHAPTER 5

ADVICE OVERLOAD

From the moment of conception an extraordinary transformation occurs in most of your family and friends. Suddenly they become expert in all aspects of pregnancy, childbirth and parenting. People who previously have come no closer to parenthood than a burst condom have a sudden burst of omniscience about stretch marks and morning sickness. Your mother, who learned a long time ago to stop offering advice on *anything*, suddenly feels it's OK to spout forth with a veritable torrent of arcane and inaccurate homilies about diet and breast care, not to mention sex and the advised cessation thereof.

Want to know what's wrong with your crying child? Go for a walk, and before long someone will stop you and say, 'Ah, your baby, she teething!' (This last often seems to come from someone of vaguely Mediterranean descent, whereas, 'Her feet are cold, she should have thicker socks' has a more Eastern European flavour.)

Just digressing on condoms and their apparent vulnerabilities for a moment – as a GP it amazes me how many young women pop in on a Monday for the morning-after pill, saying 'the condom broke ...' Are condoms really that fragile? In my limited personal experience, struggling to try and unwind one of the odious things onto a none-too-impressive and rapidly diminishing member, stretching it this way and that in a vain attempt to work out which way it unrolls, despite all the huffing and puffing and digging in of fingernails (and remember, this is just trying to get the frigging thing on ...), not one ever broke on me. Even once finally in situ, they have remained rigorously, if not rigidly, intact throughout.

I can only assume that these young things are being economical with the truth, and would prefer to say that their prophylactic split rather than confess to a bout of foolishly unprotected merriment.

But then an unsettling thought occurs, that perhaps the partners of these aforementioned young things are subjecting their cherry-flavoured sensor-lubes to a degree of protracted friction and shearing forces of which I was incapable. I reassure myself with the dishonesty hypothesis.

Everyone has an opinion, and it seems the less they know you, the more confident and extreme the opinion is likely to be. Who else but a complete stranger could possibly come up to a pregnant woman, tummy hidden under layers of clothes, and confidently predict both the due date and sex of the baby?

There's no escape – advice will come from all corners, all of it well-meaning, some of it welcome, most of it of dubious relevance. And once the baby is born, the inoffensive trickle becomes an unwelcome flood, with a redoubling of efforts by friends and families as they vie to show who's the real expert. Added to this is the input from a variety of nurses, midwives, lactation consultants, obstetricians and paediatricians.

As if this wasn't enough, what we tend to do, in this information-rich era, is seek even more advice via magazines, books, radio, TV, the internet. For every possible concern there are a dozen different sources of advice, much of it conflictual, some of it inaccurate. For a parent struggling with a crying baby, for example, this plethora of suggestions can lead to an even greater sense of loss of control and confusion.

People have managed to raise babies for tens of thousands of years in the absence of baby books or media personalities with multiple suggestions. How? Because each baby is its own self-help manual. Far from being the passive drinking, pooing and weeing machines that we sometimes think they are, babies are in fact terrific communicators right from the start. They tell us what they want with their gurgles and cries, their smiles and frowns and other responses to their environment and the people who are caring for them. Our job, as parents, is to learn the language, to find a way of interpreting these non-verbal efforts to make some kind of sense of it all. We can only do this if we trust ourselves and our baby enough.

This is where all the advice becomes dangerous. Once we start listening to 'experts', once we prefer what's written in a textbook of baby care to what our instinct and judgement tells us is right, once we assume that this particular swaddling method is 'right' or that that feeding regime is 'better', then we've stopped listening to what our baby is telling us. If we're lucky, the advice we get happens to fit for our particular baby and all goes well.

But often it doesn't, and if we then look for more advice, it may take us further away from our baby and her attempts at communicating with us. The more we rely on advice, the less we trust ourselves and the information that flows from our baby.

KIDS ARE DIFFERENT FROM THE START

My Mum is a psychologist who trained in an era when behavioural theory held sway. She was taught that babies were born with a mind that was a 'blank slate' upon which anything could be written, that is their whole personality was the result of their experiences in the world. Fifteen years and three kids later, she was finally able to say 'rubbish', kids are different right from the start. Of course, experience shapes a huge amount of what they will become, but the slate does in fact have a fair bit written on it already, before we start adding our contributions.

I saw this as a junior paediatrician treating premature babies. Despite having been born up to 10 weeks early and only weighing a kilo, they were all different. The little lamb chops, I would call them, all pink and wrinkled and tiny, but they had a personality already. In my big clumsy hands they each responded differently, as individuals.

HIGH-RISK PARENTS

Often the parents most at risk from advice overload are those who are older and better educated. Comfortable in the information age, these people (you?) are used to maintaining control of their lives through multiple sources of information. If there's a problem, there's a book somewhere, a specialist or an internet site that will have an answer. It's only natural, then, that a new event such as a baby is dealt with by searching around for information, and suddenly, boy is there a lot of it!

There's nothing wrong, of course, with the judicious use of carefully selected sources for background, interest and ideas. However, the balance sometimes tips, and when she finds herself (because it's usually mum, not dad) rummaging tearfully through the teetering pile of baby books for the solution to inconsolable screaming, you know the seesaw has bottomed out.

I can offer all sorts of possible reasons for your baby's screaming, also for her feeding problems, her sleep problems and her … Well, I guess those are the big three (see next chapter). But it's no more true that babies *should* sleep for an hour and a half twice a day from three months on than it is that they *ought* to drink 250 ml a feed. Oddly enough, babies are different, and the only one who can really tell you what your baby needs and what will work is *your baby*.

TIPS FOR TOP DADS

1. Look out for your partner using 'should' and 'ought' phrases, for example, 'She should be feeding less often than this' or 'Surely he ought to sleep more than …' These indicate expectations created by external advice, and it's worth trying to bring the focus back to the baby.

2. Encourage your partner to trust her own sense of what works and to go with those feelings.

3. Trust yourself as well – use your baby's responses to get to know what he needs. If you're not sure, don't just hand him back saying, 'He must be hungry'. Have a go. Take him out, change his nappy, sing him a song, see what happens … (which means spending time with your baby – see Chapter 7).

4. Hide or chuck out most of the baby books.

5. Don't chuck out this one.

NAPPIES

We went all 'earth-parenty' with our firstborn and used cloth nappies. Great for the environment, we thought, forgetting how we were choking the air with clouds of greenhouse gases, and our rivers with kilos of phosphates, from all the hot soapy washes.

Sanity prevailed by the time we got to number 3, but when it comes to a bit of parenting one-upmanship, nothing can beat a cloth nappy. At the next snooty parent-and-baby gathering, wait for a suitably quiet moment, pick up baby and exclaim loudly (regardless of state of current nappy) 'Boy do you need changing'. Plonk baby firmly on the carpet (under no circumstances use a change-mat – much too precious), whip off the soggy/fetid/bone-dry incumbent cloth and place rapidly in plastic bag. Next, with great flourish, pull out a spotlessly clean and fluffy cloth nappy and with great dexterity apply a three-corner bifold (if really wanting to create the full earth-father impression, substitute 'greying and frayed' for 'clean and fluffy').

Wrap skilfully around baby, hold in place with one hand and with the other, produce from baby bag a large and shiny nappy pin. Rub this ostentatiously in your hair until someone notices and asks what you're doing – respond casually 'It's for the static electricity, makes the pin much sharper'* before plunging said pin into nappy. Avoid fingers and baby's abdomen.

*Some pony-tailed parent actually told me this rot about static electricity. Rubbing the pin in your hair really does help it go through the cloth more easily, but only because you've been too exhausted to wash your hair for the last three weeks. A drop of Castrol GTX would be just as effective.

My dad is A Super Star!!!!!!!! Asher

CHAPTER 6

CRYING, SLEEPING, FEEDING

These are indeed the Big Three. If these go well, then mostly it's going to be a breeze, so let's have a look at each in turn.

CRYING

It's said that the mating call of the male koala, weighing in at around 8 kilograms, can be heard for up to 2 kilometres. I reckon many babies half that size would better than this. How can such a small package create such a penetrating, piercing sound? Amazing. But while the koala's deep-throated ursine grunting is designed to attract potential mates, your baby's screaming is more complex – and all too often, to the distress of his parents, much, much more prolonged.

It helps to know that completely healthy babies can cry for up to three hours a day. So crying, even quite a lot of crying, is not necessarily a sign of problems. Which doesn't mean shrug and ignore it until it's been going on for four hours or more – he's still trying to tell you something. Your job is to try to work out what.

This is a tricky area. Whole PhD theses have been written on the subject, not to mention any number of articles and books by people much better qualified than myself. Attempts have been made to analyse the types of cries that a baby makes, to distinguish between the cries of hunger, pain and distress, and there are plenty of suggestions out there about what to do. A Google search of 'infant' and 'crying' gives over 16 million hits, so in case you aren't already suffering from advice overload, here's your chance! Are we going to go with the 'Twelve tips for soothing your baby', or just the 'Five Ss' – Swaddling, Side/stomach positioning, Sucking, Shushing, Swinging? Do we go with babyzone.com and askdrsears.com, or more official-sounding sites like the Mayo Clinic? Or perhaps one of the thousands of Youtube videos on baby massage and soothing techniques?

Myth – Babies cry when their nappies are wet/full.

Reality – Most babies don't give two hoots what revolting state they're sloshing around in. Often, it seems the squelchier the better.

My advice? If you've read the previous chapter, you won't be surprised to hear that I'd recommend you avoid the lot. Your job is to find out what works for your baby. Does he prefer to be swaddled (wrapped up tightly) or is he more comfortable being able to move around? Does he prefer being on his side to being on his back? Is he overstimulated? I suspect this last is quite common. Sometimes the desperate parent tries one form of distraction after another – toys, mobiles, music and so on – which can be bewildering for a baby. I've seen many parents in the consulting room try to hush their crying baby by jangling a brightly coloured plastic thing in his face. Jangle jangle. 'Are you soothed yet?' A bit like tickling a parrot in front of the sniffling nose of a crying adult and expecting them to say how much better they feel.*

But even more common is the problem of understimulation.

BOREDOM AND YOUR BABY

No, this is not about what to do when you're bored with your baby, sick of the mess and dying to get out of the house – you're not going to find a list of adventure playground meeting-spots for dedicated dads, or baby-friendly cappuccino parlours in this section. This is about your baby getting bored.

---

* Actually that might work.

It may seem a strange concept, that even small babies can get bored, but it's true. They may not experience the yawn-boring-change-the-channel type of boredom that we feel as adults, but it is boredom nonetheless. Even very tiny babies are acutely aware of their surroundings, and respond to the different sights, sounds and smells that surround them. If they see, hear and smell the same things for too long, they get bored, and a baby expresses her boredom by – yes, you guessed it – crying and irritability.

'It was a horrible day – I seemed to spend the entire time trying to breastfeed her and get the washing done, but she just wouldn't settle. I was inside all day because she mucked around at the breast and wouldn't have a proper drink, so I'd try and put her down but she just grizzled and cried, so I'd put her in the bouncenette – which she normally loves – so that I could get at least the kitchen cleared up, but she wasn't happy for more than a few minutes. By the time my partner got home around 5.30 I was at my wits end ...'

There can be a bit of a vicious circle here. The irritable baby gets taken to a doctor, who diagnoses colic or reflux and suggests thickened feeds, different formulas and/or various unpalatable medications. The already frustrated parent is then left at home spending even more time with an increasingly fractious baby, trying to persuade her to swallow the noxious potions that now substitute for her usual feeds. Baby gets even more bored and frustrated, cries more, parent gets more frazzled, tears out more hair. Terrific.

This is where an awareness of the possibility of boredom can make a difference. When she's crying for reasons that are unclear, and particularly if you realise that you have been stuck at home, try getting her out and see how she responds. Whether it is a walk in a pram, a backpack, or a drive in the car doesn't matter too much; just take her out for a change of sight, sound and smell and see what happens. It can be as simple as just picking her up, wrapping her in a blanket and walking out of the house.

ROUTINES

Baby books sometimes emphasise the importance of developing routines. As with most pieces of advice, there is truth to this, but there is also a risk of becoming a slave to the routine.

Routines are no different from any other aspect of dealing with a small baby. If it's working, fine, but if not, then try and listen to what she's trying to tell you. Being stuck at home desperately trying to follow a textbook routine is a common cause of boredom, so be prepared to relax the routine and just get her out of the house. It is no coincidence that second and third babies, who may have to have their 'routines' sacrificed for the realities of the needs of the other children, are often more settled than their first-child counterparts.

HATING YOUR BABY

It's a tough business, this parenting lark. Life changes completely: there's little time for yourself, your partner's exhausted and so are you (but you're not allowed to be more exhausted than she is), and sex is a distant memory, replaced by the ever-present sound of a baby crying. A baby you're supposed to love unconditionally, but that at times you're sick to death of. A baby that, when the mewling and puking (to get all Shakespearean) becomes too much, you sometimes hate. Yes, hate.

You're normal.

Parents who have any meaningful degree of involvement with their child's care will at times feel frustrated, angry and fed up with the whole business. Inevitably there can be times when this frustration slides into a feeling of hatred. This is quite normal.

Parents are great liars. From the conversations at parents' groups you would think they all adore their children all the time. Few admit to negative thoughts, let alone to ever hating their kids. Which can leave those of us who have been in that position (i.e. most of us) feeling guilty, as if we're the only ones who have ever wanted to throw the little blighter out of the window.

Feeling hatred for your own child is never a great experience, but knowing that it's a standard and predictable part of parenting can help mitigate the guilt. Having times when you hate your child, or hate being a parent, do not make you a bad parent. They make you a normal parent.

Take a break, walk away, a few deep breaths, and remember that the good bits, the smiles and cuddles, are real too.

CAUTION

For a bloke with a short fuse, it's easy for frustration or hate to spill over into something physical – a slap or a shake perhaps. While feeling hate might be a normal and predictable part of parenting a small child, violence never is. If it's edging that way, time for help.[6]

TIPS FOR TOP DADS

1. If you're there during the day, get her (her = baby, not mother) out of the house sooner rather than later.

2. If you come home at the end of the day – the 'witching hour' for many babies – and a certain amount of witching is going on, consider getting her out of the house straight away. Hot, cold, raining – doesn't matter. Wrap her, unwrap her, whatever, she doesn't care: just get her out. The pipe and slippers can wait.

3. Don't worry if she's got a cold/just had a vaccination/is teething. Often in these situations they've been stuck at home even more, and fresh air, even if cold and wet, will only do her good.

SLEEPING

Recently I was talking to some new parents, and I asked where their baby slept. Mum looked sheepishly at dad and told me, as if confessing a guilty secret, 'In bed with us'. There was a short pause, the air heavy with expectation, as if they awaited my judgement. It took me straight back to the school principal's office, on one of my occasional visits after some minor misdemeanour (such as the time we chucked the Latin master's Mini in the school pond. Really. He deserved it.) Except that this time I was the principal:

'You look as if you expect me to disapprove?'

(Apologetically) 'Well, we hadn't planned to have her in our bed, in fact we were told we shouldn't, but it seems to work …'

'So what's the problem? Does it work for both of you?'

(Cautious smiles and nodding) 'Well yes, it does…'

'And do you know how to do it safely?'

'Yes, I've read everything there is about it.'

'Well that should be fine then, but let's go through it in some detail to make sure.'

(My principal was never that understanding. We got six of the best. Really.)

Note the 'should' word in there. These eminently sensible parents were feeling bad because they had been told what their baby should, or in this case shouldn't, do and they had had the temerity to do the opposite. Shock, horror, shudder.

The current advice is that the best place for babies to sleep is in their own cot beside the parents' bed. There is some evidence that this is the safest way, so it's a good idea to start this way if possible. Babies can sleep in a cot in their own rooms, in a cot in the parents' room, or, if it feels right to you, in the parents' bed. All of these can be OK so long as they work for you and your baby, but there are a few suggestions and even one or two rules.

POSITION

Sudden Infant Death Syndrome (SIDS – what used to be called cot death) has been shown to be more likely if babies sleep on their fronts or sides, so try to get her to sleep on her back. Most babies are happy to do this, so position her on her back right from the start. Funny how things change, though – when I worked in paediatrics, back in the Dark Ages (1983), we were told babies should sleep on their fronts.

TOYS, PILLOWS AND OTHER STUFF

This is your first baby, so you were given 13 teddies, four knitted quilts, two embroidered cot bumpers and umpteen assorted pillows, cushions and soft toys. Lovely, but not in the cot, as they can get over her head and smother her. Keep it simple – just a firm mattress covered with a tight-fitting sheet and a top sheet/ blanket well tucked in.

SMOKING

You don't, do you? Thought not. And even if you did, I wouldn't really have to tell you not to smoke around your baby, would I?

CO-SLEEPING

By this I mean having your baby in your bed, not just in the bedroom. A popular choice in some societies, and there are experts who believe that babies who co-sleep actually do better. A few years ago I interviewed Professor James McKenna on the ABC.[7] He's one of the enthusiasts who says that co-sleeping with a breastfed baby is not only OK, but that it may help the little one develop certain strengths, such as stronger independence, more social competence, higher self-esteem and stronger sexual identity.[8] I don't think too many of us would complain about those outcomes for our kids.

At a more mundane level, co-sleeping can certainly ease the burden of night-time feeding, as your baby can feed on demand while mum stays warm and snug. But there are also organisations that are concerned that co-sleeping in Western-style bedding is unsafe, so it's a tricky area with no absolute right answer.

Personally, I completely understand why people enjoy co-sleeping. Babies are such wonderfully warm, snuggly little creatures, and if I were mum, I wouldn't want to tramp down a cold corridor several times a night either. If you do decide to co-sleep, here are some rules to make it as safe as possible:

> Smoking increases the risk of SIDS if you co-sleep. Don't ask me why, it's just a fact. If either of you smokes, don't co-sleep.
> Avoid alcohol and drugs that can make you sleep too heavily. Again, there's a proven increased risk of SIDS.

> Keep your baby's head away from pillows, and preferably avoid heavy doonas that risk overheating.
> Make sure your baby can't get stuck in an enclosed space, such as between the mattress and a wall or headboard.
> Always have her sleeping on her back.

This is a complex and changing area, so I'd strongly recommend you seek updated advice from one of the many reputable internet sites, such as <http://raisingchildren.net.au>.

SETTLING

I was so besotted with our first baby that I carried him around all the time, and used to rock and sing him to sleep, which is yet another thing I 'shouldn't' have done. Such a failure as a parent, so much guilt ... NO! It felt right at the time, I loved it, he seemed not to mind too much, and 22 years later he doesn't hate me. But maybe it did take him longer to learn to settle himself as a result. So, if possible, put your baby in her cot awake so that she begins to learn to settle herself. It might help her if you spend a minute or two patting or singing to her to help calm her, but try not to spend too long doing this, as it teaches her that she needs you there. I've known parents who spend 20, 30 or more minutes settling at every sleep, which is exhausting.

CRYING AT SLEEP TIME

'Just leave her to cry, she'll stop eventually.'

I've heard this said any number of times, and you might have too. Yes she'll stop eventually: exhausted, confused, frightened and uncertain. Probably not how we'd like her to feel.

That doesn't mean she shouldn't be allowed to cry at all when going to sleep. It's that balance thing again. Some babies need to cry for a bit, but she also needs to know that you're there and can offer comfort, even if the comfort doesn't necessarily stop her crying. As with so much with tiny babies, there's no magic formula – trust your instinct.

DAYTIME SLEEPS

We modern Westerners can get a bit precious about daytime sleeps. (Actually we can get a bit precious about the whole baby thing, but I've got to be a bit careful. If you and I weren't at least a *bit* precious about it, I wouldn't be writing this, and you wouldn't be reading it. But as usual, I digress …) How many should she have, how long should they be, how to develop a routine, how many sleep cycles and so on. But keep in mind that the human female has a natural fecundity* of around 12 to 14 babies. What this means is that, given no restrictions (the Pill, reluctant partner, inability to afford a minibus, common sense, etc.), a sexually active woman will have that number of babies in her reproductive lifetime. The natural state for most human babies then was to have to make do amongst a sea of siblings. Not too many routines there.

This remains true today for second and subsequent babies, who get used to being lumped off in the pram for a trip to kinder or

---

* This always sounds to me like a bit of a dirty word. Fecundity. Hmm. It's the potential number of offspring of a species, similar to fertility.

library music-time. They sleep when they can, and it works just fine.

So my preference is not to worry too much about daytime sleeps, but to see what evolves. As with everything with a new baby, they're quite good at letting you know whether it's working. Our first needed a bit more structure, and he made this quite clear – if he didn't get into his cot when he was tired, he would rapidly become a screaming monster. The girls were a bit easier. But we didn't know any of this until they 'told' us.

FEEDING

A baby is an incredible device for converting milk into a human being. Which really is rather extraordinary when you think about it – all that person, all those different bits of brain and lung and kidney and skin and bone and everything else, being created entirely from this single white substance. That's some pretty clever chemistry.

Preferably, it should be white substance from the breast. Breastfeeding is great, and you've had enough people telling you that it's the right way to go, so you don't need me to add to the chorus. So long as it's working well, go for it. Your job, Dad, is to support mum in every way possible so that she has the best chance to breastfeed. Provide water, cups of chamomile tea or whatever, lots of encouragement, turn down AC/DC and go and make dinner. Job done.

But I have also seen women tortured by trying to breastfeed. Women for whom, despite everything they've tried, it just does not work. We're fortunate that we have an alternative, and while bottle feeding should not be our first preference, it's way up there ahead of starvation. If it all becomes too much and the decision is to try the bottle, time to switch allegiance and help her feel OK about this. And it gives you a chance to do some of the night-time feeds.

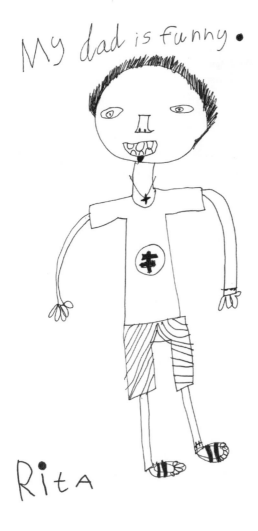

CHAPTER 7
TIME

'Bye, darling, sorry I have to rush, but I've got to be there early today. I should be back by seven ...'

Time can be one of the toughest and yet most important issues for the new father. Many of us find ourselves embarking on fatherhood at a stage when jobs and careers are becoming increasingly demanding. Often there are other demands too. You've just moved interstate with the new job; taken out a rather too-large mortgage; the architect has some wonderful (= expensive) ideas about how you could renovate; the boss makes encouraging noises about how, with a bit of hard work and dedication, you could have a great future; and so, because there doesn't seem to be enough occupying your attention at the moment, you decide to have a baby.

Someone once pointed out that there are 168 hours in the week and we all get them. Sometimes, though, it feels like we've been short-changed, and this is often true for new fathers. 'I just don't seem to have the time' is a common refrain, with 'There's nothing I can do about it, I have no choice' a close second.

Many of us had the experience of fathers who weren't around much, who were busy being hard at work and not having enough time. Many of us have even said on their behalf, 'He had no choice'. The reality for men who say this about their own fathers is that most recognise that they would have liked more time from their dads. They may even suspect that the lack of time spent together is one of the main reasons that they feel disconnected from their fathers.

So time is important. Very important. Time is so important that it's worth using some of it to think and plan about it. Even before your baby is born, think about how much time you will have. How much time would you *like* to have? Is there anything you can do to make more time? No? *Really* no? I don't believe you – think laterally, think radically. What would happen if you asked for a day off a week? If you went part-time? If you changed your job? If you stopped work? The best decision I ever made was to give up one day's work a week. I had a whole weekday at home to look after first one, then two, then three kids. Hard work? Yes. Boring? Sometimes. Regretted? Never.

Too radical? Perhaps, but then so is the concept of really enjoying being a father. It's such a cliché, but there really is nothing in life that can bring the same rewards as the close bond between a parent and child; yet somehow dads often seem to stroll into fatherhood expecting to glimpse their children before and after work during the week, and between golf rounds at the weekends. They are then puzzled when they feel less than fulfilled as a father and/or feel no connection with their teenagers. Sorry, Dad, you may be a great guy, but unless you do something to make some more time available, that's how it's likely to be.

NO TEENAGER EVER TURNED AROUND AND SAID, 'GEE DAD, THANKS FOR SPENDING ALL THOSE HOURS AT THE OFFICE'.

THE MYTH OF QUALITY TIME

The idea that you can compensate for working 12 hour days and every other weekend by spending 'quality time' with the kids is one of the most destructive myths of modern parenting. Of course kids love doing 'activities' with you – whether it's painting, drawing, reading or whatever – but a short burst of this kind of interaction cannot possibly substitute for your participation in the more mundane hustle and bustle of normal domestic life. Twenty minutes of 'quality time', instead of having breakfast together, getting them dressed and organised for the day, going to the supermarket together, putting them down for a daytime sleep and being there when they wake up again, simply does not work. Sure, kids need interaction; just being there reading the paper or watching the news doesn't count. Sometimes you may choose to do things together that would be called 'quality time' activities, which is great, but they are not sufficient in themselves. ***The only really quality time is quantity time.***

BATH TIME

All babies need a bath, and it is one of the few things for a newborn that:

> they enjoy, and
> can be done by either parent, and
> is also fun for the parent (as opposed to changing nappies)

But then, all too often I hear that mum does most of the bath times.

'*… the baby bath's in the laundry; yes, the baby soap's there too, and the towels are with the clean nappies … No, don't fill it from the kettle! You could scald him, and if you're not careful the sheepskin's going to … Oh for heaven's sakes let me do it!*'

Here's a top-dad tip – you do bath time. All the time. And here's another tip – don't wait until the end of the day, when you're tired and your baby's fractious; have bath time in the morning.

If your experience with your new baby is anything like ours, nights in the first few weeks are not great. Lots of crying, feeding, nappy changes, and by 6 am, a marital bed that looks like the seven dwarfs just held a party in it. Various small items of clothing randomly scattered; uncertain plastic items under the doona that have an adults-only feel, but that on closer inspection could once have been attached to dummies or bottles; an exhausted, tousled, partially dressed Snow White asleep; and somewhere, a little person whose fleeting dwarf-like appearance clears when you rub your eyes and realise it's your baby.

Our way of dealing with this? When our baby woke in the morning, my wife would give him a feed, and then I would take him out of the bedroom, leaving her to finally sink into real, baby-free sleep. Into the kitchen we'd go, heater cranked up in winter, some soothing music. (James Taylor seemed to suit the occasion – my apologies to my now adult son. Not quite Wolfmother, I know, but you really did love it at the time!) I'd fill the baby bath, and off we'd go, water sloshing everywhere as limbs thrashed joyfully. And if the CD needed changing and he slipped under the water for just a moment, who was to know?

OK, I'm kidding about that last bit, but the principle applies. Soap would get in his mouth, shampoo in his eyes, water in his mouth, but we managed, we had fun, he survived. We did it our way, and in the end he was cleaner and we were both happy. Then onto the sheepskin, lots of towels to wrap him up, and there he'd be as I got on with breakfast. Then into the bathroom, and there he'd be as I performed my morning ablutions.*

The final step – get him dressed, get myself dressed, then deliver a clean, contented and hungry baby to a still-tousled but less exhausted mum. A good feed and within minutes he would be fast asleep, giving her the chance to shower and organise herself without interruption. And hi-ho, off to work I'd go.

Beautiful. You might want to try it.

ANYONE FOR TENNIS? TIME FOR YOURSELF ...

You can't be the great dad and partner that you want to be unless you also look after yourself. That means negotiating at least some time and space in your week which is for you. Personally, I've always played sport of one kind or another (Real Tennis anyone?). When I became a dad, my wife, who was of course amazing, wonderful and incomparable in every other respect,** not infrequently expected me to cancel a regular tennis game for one or another domestic imperative. Grudgingly I would comply, until I realised I was getting a bit toey about it. Eventually I worked out why:

---

* An experience that continued for many years afterwards, not just with him, but subsequently with both daughters. It wasn't a big bathroom, so it used to be pretty busy in there, and as for privacy – ha! And to think my own father used to sit on the toilet in splendid isolation long enough to do *The Times* crossword ...

** It's unlikely she'll ever read this, but you never know ...

(Me): 'I don't need to go and talk to someone, but I do need to run around and hit things. It keeps me fit, it keeps me feeling good. It's not just a luxury, some kind of optional extra; it's my therapy.' (This last was the clincher – she's a psychotherapist, she gets the therapy bit.)

'Oh darling, I hadn't realised! You're right, of course, and your sound psychological health is just as important to me as maintaining your impressive physique and six-pack.' (This is a work of fiction, right?)

A couple I know are mad-keen cyclists. They are in the fortunate position that both of them are bitten by the same bug, so neither has to explain to the other why they 'need' to ride. They rarely get to hit the road together, but they understand the importance for each to have the space to do so individually. One of those rare occasions when the phrase 'On yer bike' is a positive. Oh, if it were always like that!

But the conversation above did make a difference; she became less grudging, I became less guilty and we both felt better.

As with everything, there's a balance. Working five days a week, then saying you need to play golf all weekend is probably pushing the therapy line a little too far. But all of us need some 'me' time, and finding a way to make this possible for each of you will make parenting a lot more enjoyable.

CHAPTER 8

SEX AND YOUR PARTNER

Men are wankers.

No, this is not the start of some anti-male diatribe written by a sociology major. It's a statement of fact. Research has shown that 99 per cent of men have, at some time in their lives, masturbated. (Now *there's* valuable research for you – I'd never have known …) Research also shows that 1 per cent of men are liars.

For most men (and probably for women too, but not really my field of expertise), teenage experimentation with masturbation was variously furtive, hurried, guilt-ridden, discovered, denied, taboo; perhaps even punished. As single teenagers we became experts at snatching our moments of secret pleasure. There is also plenty of research to show that men in active sexual relationships, including marriage, are not averse to the occasional solo effort.

'So what?' I hear the cry. Fair question; after all, your partner's pregnant, so it hasn't *all* been mopped up with some soggy tissues behind a locked door. But there are various harsh realities of pregnancy and parenting, which include:

> Early pregnancy – she's got morning (or all day) nausea
> Late pregnancy – she's feeling heavy, tired, dyspeptic, BIG
> Early parenting – exhaustion, she's breastfeeding 23½ hours a day
> Later parenting – exhaustion, kids in same bed
> Later still – exhaustion, kids still there.

Etc …

You may have been lucky enough to have had times of frequent, wild, uninhibited sex; passionate at the sight of each other, falling into a limb-locked embrace every time the adverts come on. If so, I keep my fingers crossed for you, in the fond hope that you will revisit such times.

Sadly, the condition that such activity has now got your partner into results in some or all of the less lust-inducing feelings listed above. A woman whose stomach is behaving as if she's on the Sydney-to-Hobart yacht race in a 40-knot southerly usually feels the fire of passion burning somewhat feebly. At 38 weeks, many women feel they must have been impregnated not by you, but by an elephant. Just turning over in bed is a major achievement, and the last thing she wants is you jumping all over her as well. And after the baby is born ... well, how do you think you'd react if someone came along and suggested some riotous sexual intercourse while you still felt as if someone had just driven a double-decker bus through your vagina?

Yes, parenting and sex: whereas the latter is usually the cause of the former, the former then often seems to prevent the latter – if you see what I mean.

SEX AFTER PREGNANCY

There are also the many and often confusing feelings that men have, once their partner is pregnant. Will I hurt her? Could I hurt the baby? It's all so different; she doesn't seem to want me any more; she doesn't smell the same now she's living on Twisties and spring onions ...

The reality is that, whatever your sex life was like pre-pregnancy, it's likely to change once pregnancy ensues, and one of the commonest changes is long spells when you *don't* have sex. These spells may be weeks, they may be months. For many men they are longer than their natural cycles of desire can survive. In this case, for the periods between sexual contact with your partner, there are basically only four options:

1. Hang on
2. Wet dreams

3. Sex elsewhere

4. Masturbation.

Rather a stark list, isn't it? Option one works for a while, but can lead to option two, which may not be all that welcome. It's pretty hard to explain when, for the first time in a five-year relationship, *you* strip the bed and wash the sheets.

You might say the same about option four. After all, that's why we grew up and started things like relationships. Wet dreams and wanking are kids' stuff. But check out option three – dynamite!

Yes, dynamite. Option three could well blow everything to bits.

It might seem superficially a more attractive proposal, but let's have a bit of a reality check here. You have a pregnant partner, you're going to have a baby to care for and enjoy together (that is the idea, isn't it?) and you'd quite like that little person to have *two* parents to grow up with. Funnily enough, accomplishing this will cause quite a few changes and one of the things that will change, at some point and for some time, is your sex life. It is essential that you understand this and don't look outside your relationship to ease your sexual frustrations.

This is not a question of morality so much as a practical point – morality is fluid and depends on the individual, whereas the practicalities are more universal. By accepting the inevitability of a change in your sex life, and that you will deal with this 'in-house', you join with your partner in one of the vicissitudes of procreation. Which is a fancy way of saying that having a kid throws up some tough shit, but you'll cope.

You accept that things are not all to your liking and that there are (here comes the word) SACRIFICES to be made. Not sacrifices in the sense of some sort of daft martyrdom, noble but pointless, but in the sense of working together towards a common goal. If you can say, 'Our sex life is different, and it doesn't really suit me at the moment, but it's tough for her too and we need to get through this together', things are beginning to sound pretty healthy.

If, on the other hand, your reaction is more like, 'Bugger this for a joke, let's see what else is out there' you immediately risk splitting yourself from the shared role you were planning to undertake together – and that's even if she *doesn't* find out and you get away with it.

Let's turn it around the other way. Let's suppose that the method of reproduction is different and that you get to carry the baby. 'Oh, darling', she says, 'I love you and want you to have our baby'. 'Oh, OK' you reply – and within a few weeks you're beginning to feel sick, your chest is expanding, you're getting stretch marks on your previously washboard abs, and your diet consists mainly of lemonade icy poles. Sometimes at night the nausea settles long enough for you not to repel her advances, but mostly you turn your back rather apologetically and feel guilty. Nearing the time for delivery she seems a bit more understanding – anyway, the bed's so full of pregnancy pillows for your tummy, hot water bottles for your backache and books on natural childbirth that she can't get near you. After the baby's born, and you finally get home, weeks pass in a fug of milk and shattered sleep. Fortunately, she doesn't seem to mind; she hasn't been starting those tentative advances that so distressed you before – and then you find out why. While you've been going through all this, your body and your life being pulled apart and reconstructed, she's been having an affair with another man.

You don't feel too terrific about this.

It wouldn't be great, would it? In fact, it's hard to think of a situation where you'd feel more betrayed.

So what should we do? I don't think there is an easy answer other than *not* to take the easy answer – that is, option three.

One favourite suggestion from the 'experts' is to go back to a bit of old-fashioned wooing. Create the space for some time together: cook her a special dinner, light candles, open good wine, scatter the evening liberally with rose petals, compliments and chocolates, and await the outcome. Which is likely to be a grateful smile and an early night. A friend related the following story from a men's group: the young blokes were bemoaning the lack of sex and expressing doubt that wooing would work. An older Russian father had this to say: 'You young things, you no idea. I tell you what you do. You buy bunch of flowers, you take her out to dinner. You woo her. After dinner, maybe you get f***, maybe you just get bunch flowers. But she happy.' Spot on.

I think for most men it's a question of surviving on whatever combination of the sex you can reasonably enjoy together and options one, two and four. This is perhaps where you put into practice some of that masturbatory expertise that you spent so many of your younger years developing.

Do you talk to your partner about it? I doubt that many men do, or that it would be a very comfortable conversation on either side if tried. Fine if you can, but discussing the details of what's going on, how often, where and when, is not necessarily the point. The point is for you to understand that, even if nothing is said, she will be acutely aware that the torrent of your usual sex life has slowed to a trickle, and that she will be worried. What she needs to know is:

1. That you're OK, you're managing.
2. That even if you and her are not actually having sex at the moment, you still find her sexually attractive. If you're not having sex, and you don't say anything, she *won't* know this, so you have to tell her. You have to tell her (truthful) things about what you like about her, complimenting her when you like the way she looks. She's changed physically and will feel uncertain about how you feel – you need to tell her.
3. An acknowledgement that sex isn't top priority for either of you at the moment, and that that's OK.

She doesn't need to know what you actually *are* doing, except if she's wondering what else you *might* be up to; in which case you might choose to allude to whatever means of relief are to hand, so to speak. (Mind you, if she reads this chapter you may end up having to discuss it, so make sure you leave the bookmark in the chapter about nappies or something equally uncontroversial. And speaking of bookmarks, be discreet about the websites you visit.)

What is undoubtedly true is that if you can get through these early stages together, keeping as much physical closeness as you are able while maintaining the communication (a healthy sense of humour helps enormously), you stand a much better chance of revitalising your sex life in the future. Together.

PHYSICAL FACTS

In case you missed it, her body's changed. What were once erogenous zones, existing solely for her (and your) arousal, have become utilitarian outlets for a life-sustaining fluid. Yes, I'm talking nipples here. Imagine if your penis were suddenly transformed into a milk dispenser. Confusing? Creepy? It certainly can be confusing for her (and yes, some women get an erotic response to breastfeeding, even at times to the point of orgasm). She may be happy to share her milk dispensers between the baby and you, but she may well not. Don't just dive in on them like before, but equally don't simply avoid them at all costs, as if they have suddenly transformed into some foreign and vaguely threatening species – ask!

Vaginal lubrication is often much reduced, particularly when breastfeeding (it's a hormone thing), so don't be in too much of a rush. Your focus may be on that one bit of your own anatomy, but chances are her focus is less genital. More foreplay, lots of stroking of the bits she wants stroked, and remember that, even though you may be gagging for the home run, she may not be. If at the end of all this stroking and massaging you are both still awake, accept whatever is on offer with good grace.

CHAPTER 9

HEALTH MISCELLANY

REFLUX

We've always had a 'label' or diagnosis for the baby who cries a lot. When I did my paediatric training, back in the early 1980s, 'colic' was on the way out and 'reflux' was on the way in. Today, it seems that any baby who cries for more than a few minutes is said to be possibly suffering from reflux. And one of the treatments for reflux is medication.

Well, yes, reflux is a real condition and can certainly cause crying, but just as there are black swans, there are plenty of babies whose crying has nothing to do with reflux.* A wonderful piece of research by Associate Professor Brigid Jordan at the Royal Children's Hospital in Melbourne looked at babies with proven reflux.[9] Even for the babies with the most severe reflux, as measured by acid monitoring in the gullet, there was no correlation between the degree of reflux and symptoms such as crying, back arching or feeding difficulties.

WHAT IS REFLUX?

At the junction between the gullet (oesophagus) and the stomach is a muscular valve whose job it is to stop stomach contents coming back up into the gullet. The stomach environment is very acidic, and if anything gets back up past the valve, it can hurt the gullet. This is called reflux. Many adults have experienced it. It's common for women during pregnancy, as the pressure of the baby in the abdomen makes the valve work less well.

In babies the valve is less effective anyway, and all babies reflux to some extent – think of how easily babies posset (bring up some milk) or fully vomit compared to older kids or adults. For some babies the acid from the stomach frequently refluxes back into the gullet. This may be enough to hurt, so they cry and become more irritable.

---

* Alright, alright Mr Pedantic, the analogy isn't strictly correct. It should be, 'Just as there are white things that aren't swans...', but that loses the Australian flavour. For those unfamiliar with the original assertion, the (inaccurate) logic was: 'All swans are white. That is white, therefore it is a swan.'

Importantly, the treatment of reflux does not *have* to be medication. In the abovementioned research, the good professor took the babies with ordinary baby reflux and allocated them to one of three groups. One group received medication, the other placebo (inactive, or dummy, medication), the third counselling for the mothers. The results? All three groups did equally well. Medication helped, but no more than the placebo, and if anything the counselling helped even more.

So where does that leave the parent who has been told their baby has reflux? If your baby is really unsettled and irritable, get her checked out to make sure there's nothing else wrong. If it seems like reflux, and medication feels like the right way to go, that's fine. But I think it helps to know that it's not the only or necessary way of helping. In my many years of seeing unsettled babies, I have very rarely had to prescribe reflux medication. What do we do instead? We try to get a better feel of what it is that the baby is trying to tell us by her crying – see Chapter 6.

WHEN TO TAKE YOUR CHILD TO THE DOCTOR

I was once asked to give a talk at the local Maternal and Child Health Centre with this title. I said I was happy to do so, but it would be very short, as the answer is, 'When you're worried'. There is no exact temperature, amount of crying, type of rash and so on which can tell you when to get your child checked. Trust your gut feeling; if you're concerned, or just not sure, go and see your doctor. This is also how you learn, and as time goes by you'll have a better sense of when to seek help. For me as a

GP there is never a problem checking a child and being able to say things are OK, nothing serious.

Also, kids can change very quickly. A baby who was feverish and crying at 5 in the morning can look robustly normal when finally seen at 10.45 am. Any experienced doctor knows this. The fact that the patient is now gurgling happily in his pram and smiling cherubically at everyone in the waiting room does not mean that the frantic phone call asking for an appointment at short notice was silly, and you should never be made to feel that way.

DUMMIES FOR DUMMIES?

Another one of those parenting issues that produces strong, and diametrically opposed, views. I remember not wanting to ever use them, out of some vague but completely unformulated idea that they were 'bad', or at least 'not good'. I also remember walking around at 3 in the morning with our firstborn sucking peacefully on my little finger and thinking, 'Don't they make something that does this?' The next day I went out and bought five dummies and our nights were transformed thereafter.

Curiously, neither of the next two kids ever wanted to use a dummy, though it was offered.

Was it bad for him? Was it better for the other two not to have had them? I have no proof either way, other than to say that all three are happy, healthy adults now. He was what I call a 'sucky' baby right from the start – loved the breast, his bottles, his dummies and derived great pleasure and comfort from them all.

It worked for him; the girls didn't seem to have the same need. And over time, he gave them up without any great struggle.

What does the research tell us? In the case of dummies, nothing very definite. There have been concerns that dummy use might interfere with breastfeeding, cause ear infections, nipple confusion* and even cot death. Fortunately there is no proof that any of this is true.

So my suggestion is, if you think your baby would benefit from a dummy, try it and see if it helps. As with all things, there's a balance – I'm not a big fan of seeing thumping great three-year-olds running around permanently 'plugged' (though I know of no major harm from this, despite what the dentists might say). But as a soother and comforter – not for nothing do the Americans call them pacifiers – when a child is fractious or due for a sleep, they can be a big help. For child *and* parent.

NAPPY CHANGING

Changing a girl's nappy requires a few simple precautions. Be aware that normal healthy poo contains a bacterium – E. Coli – which can cause urinary infections. It's a good idea therefore to try and clean all the poo away from the vaginal area, and to do so by wiping back towards the anus, away from the urethra. You

---

* 'Nipple confusion' is a slightly odd technical term. It refers to the difficulty babies may have going back to sucking at the breast (which requires different mouth muscles) after sucking something like a bottle or dummy. It doesn't mean your baby will suddenly look perplexed when presented with the breast.

don't have to go overboard though. A few flecks of poo left in the vagina will do no harm and will come out on their own. On the other hand, obsessively wiping and trying to forage out every last morsel risks causing irritation, which can lead to labial adhesions (see p. 74). A sensible clean, front to back, and a little nappy cream to soothe any sore bits is all that is needed.

Boys? Piece of cake. Urine infection is much less likely, as the E. Coli are not so good at finding their way down a penis and into the bladder. Clean, cream, wrap, done.

THE GROT THEORY

It's real name is the Hygiene Hypothesis, but I prefer the Grot Theory. It's the suggestion that some of the health problems plaguing Westernised society – such as asthma, eczema, allergies, diabetes – may be partly because our lifestyles have become too clean, too sterile. The theory is that our immune systems do not have to deal with as much dirt and germs as they used to and, being under-used, then trigger illness. Maybe life needs to be a bit grottier.

I was a lazy parent, who could never be bothered to properly sterilise anything. If the dummy fell out and into the cat's food bowl, it would get a cursory wipe and be replugged. So this is my kind of theory.

It's always made sense to me. Were the yak bones sterilised before they were given to little cave babies to gnaw on? Probably not. Babies suck everything: nipples, bottles, dummies, that old blanket you last washed in 2009, yak bones when available, and the reflex to stick everything in their mouths stays over the first year. For every bit of careful sterilising you've done, there's a germ-laden object heading into her mouth RIGHT NOW!

So relax. Sterilise when you must; otherwise just wipe off the obvious dirt/mould/anything that on close inspection looks like it might be moving and get on with life. And just think – your casual approach to hygiene could be responsible for her robust good health later in life.

WILL OUR CAT KILL THE BABY?

We acquired our first cat, a gorgeous Burmese, from a family who had just had their first baby. 'He'll smother the baby, keep him outside', they'd been told. They tried. The cat yowled, in that piercing baby-like way that only Oriental cats can, and the new mother's breasts would leak copiously in response. Everyone, human and feline alike, was miserable. So we got the cat.

Then we had our first baby. We were told the same – he'll smother the baby or, more bizarrely, he'll 'suck the breath from your baby'. Gosh, wouldn't want that. I checked with a leading surgeon at the Royal Children's Hospital in Melbourne, who went through the records – no case of a cat killing a baby that he could find. Since then, I have never seen a single case described where this was confirmed as having happened.

Animals are great for kids. They also contribute to the Grot Theory (see above). If there were any provable risk, I wouldn't have let the cat near my lot. But I had no concerns and I don't think you should either.

WHAT ABOUT THE DOG?

I have an ancient arthritic terrier of thoroughly mixed heritage who is a complete wimp. Brush him too firmly and he yelps as if his leg is being amputated. Rusty is so gentle I sometimes take him to help out in my consulting room. (He curls up on a chair and enchants the kids.) But I would never, ever leave him alone with a baby or small child. Why? Not because he has ever shown the remotest sign of doing anything more threatening than roll over to have his tummy rubbed, but because he is an animal, and animals can do unpredictable things. Many of the appalling stories of dog attacks on babies and toddlers have been by trusted household pets.

So, does Puddles the poodle have to go? Back to the pound for Hamlet?* No. There are some simple things you can do to prepare your dog for the arrival of what is, for Flossie, a small, rival, noisy but curiously immobile puppy-like thing. Ensuring that Flossie is well-trained and obedient is critical, but dog behaviour is not really my expertise. If you want to know more, check out the RSPCA website for lots of useful information and links.[10]

But the one absolute rule is: do not leave your baby alone with the dog. Ever.

'NORMAL' ODDITIES

There are all sorts of things that parents notice about their babies that can cause concern, but most of which are quite

---

* Great Dane – what else?

normal or innocent variations. Here are just a few of them, starting from the top and working down. Oh, and this advice is, of course, of a general nature. If any of the following doesn't seem to quite fit for your baby, see your doctor. That applies whenever something doesn't feel right (see 'When to take your child to the doctor', p. 64).

BLUE MARK ACROSS THE NOSE

Commonly a small vein runs at an angle across the bridge of the nose, giving a blueish appearance. Normal, and fades with time.

ACNE-LIKE RASH ON THE FACE

There are several common rashes that newborns get on their faces, and over half of all healthy babies will get some form of facial rash. Many will get an acne-like rash with red spots that can also look like pustules (pimples). In a healthy baby, this is normal and resolves without any treatment over the first month or two. Do not squeeze the spots, dad.

Some are more like red dots (miliaria, like heat rash) or white/yellow dots (milia). Both of these also normally settle in the first month or two without treatment.

There are many other versions of rash, including forms of dermatitis, cradle cap and so on. One of my favourites is the so-called 'stork bite' mark. This is a small pink or reddish patch which may be found on the back of the baby's neck at the base of the skull, or on the front of her face on the eyelids, between the eyes, or occasionally on the upper lip. The lovely name arises because the mark is from where the stork (which as you know carried your baby safely to you) picked her up.* It is caused by an area of immature blood vessels and sometimes looks more angry when he is crying. Like most of the other rashes, these fade and disappear on their own. If there is any doubt, check with your doctor.

LUMPS ON THE HEAD

There are a couple of lymph nodes that parents sometimes find that concern them. One is behind the ear, the other on the back part of the head, about halfway between the top of the ear and the very back of the head. They feel like soft, ovoid lumps under the skin, are not tender at all, and are completely normal.

TONGUE-TIE

There is a thin membrane under the tongue. Have a look in the mirror – put your tongue on the roof of your mouth and you should see it there, on the underside of your tongue. Frenulum is its proper medical name, and in newborns it can be close to the tip of the tongue. In extreme cases, it stops the tongue tip from moving forward, which can interfere with feeding, and subsequently speech. This is so-called tongue-tie (unlike when you were 15 and that gorgeous girl from the year ahead stood next to you on the school bus – that's a different form of tongue-tie. Surgery is less effective in this case).

---

* I explained to a lovely Brazilian couple that the funny red thing on the back of their baby's neck was a stork-bite mark. They looked at me uncomprehendingly. I'm not sure what animal brings the South American babies, but I suspect it's not a stork.

A quick, simple, safe and (relatively) painless solution for young babies is to snip the frenulum – done by a surgeon, not you – no anaesthetic required. But, like many things in nature, left alone it will often resolve as the tongue grows past the frenulum, so delay the snip unless severely affected.

FUNNY SHAPED HEADS

Try squeezing an egg into a milk bottle. (Remember them?) Yup, it's either going to get stuck or, more likely, break. Now think about a baby's head and its excursion down the birth canal. Big head, narrow passage – definitely an egg-and-milk-bottle scenario if the baby's head were a fixed structure like an eggshell. But, as I'm sure you know, it is not. The bones of the skull are made so they can slide over each other, which is why babies can come out looking a very strange shape indeed. Fortunately, after birth they quickly change to looking more like a real baby, less like a crushed walnut.

But the skull remains malleable for many months (there's a brain in there that has to get bigger, remember?), so can easily change shape again. If, for example, your baby sleeps only flat on her back, her head can end up looking flattened or asymmetrical.* This can be a major cause of anxiety for parents.

Fortunately, the general answer is that you needn't be anxious, as the head is very good at remodelling itself as time goes by, and usually without any parental intervention. Parents are often advised to try to make their baby lie in a different position, or

---

* But then, didn't your doctor tell you she should *only* sleep on her back? Oh yes.

have more tummy time. My suggestion? By all means have a gentle go, but don't overdo it. Trying to force her to change is likely to make her fractious, and anyway is usually unnecessary. And please do not rush off to a cranio-osteopath for a 'readjustment' ... Mostly you don't need to do anything at all apart from wait.

TUMMY BUTTONS

OK, umbilicus if you want to get all medical. Two common 'problems' can occur here, one which requires treatment, the other which usually doesn't. Let's go with the second one first.

UMBILICAL HERNIA

This is a soft sausage-like swelling from the umbilicus itself which can be pushed back in, but then pops out again. It can get larger during crying, which sometimes looks a bit alarming – is it going to pop? (No.) It is caused by a natural defect in the abdominal wall where the umbilical cord attached and did its life-giving stuff.

In pre-decimal England, it was traditional to treat these by strapping a penny over the bulge. Creative, arcane and useless. In African kids, herniae like these are very common, and for boys it is said that the bigger the hernia, the bigger the manhood. Not sure what the deal is for the girls, but it serves to illustrate that these herniae are not regarded as a medical problem. Mostly they close up and resolve themselves within the first year or two; only rarely do they require surgery.

GRANULOMA

Another common problem is a pink fleshy growth on the umbilicus which appears in the first weeks of life, soon after the dead remnant of cord falls off. It looks a bit like a tiny strawberry, and is called a granuloma. It doesn't matter too much, but is easily treated by your local doctor, so get her to have a look.

LABIAL ADHESIONS

It is common for girl babies to develop a thin membrane between the inner vaginal lips. This is called labial adhesion. It is not present at birth, but often starts around three months of age, and probably affects around 2 per cent of girls. It usually starts at the back of the vaginal opening, nearer the anus, and moves forward towards the clitoris and urethra. The membrane may therefore cover only a part, or sometimes all, of the vaginal opening.

No one quite knows why it happens, but we think it is due to irritation around the vagina, possibly from nappy contents, or soaps and perfumes and so on.

Concerning though this may sound, worry not. As she gets older and starts moving around more, the membrane tends to break down and disappear. Even if it doesn't, it eventually goes at the start of puberty, when her natural oestrogens help the membrane break down. So doing nothing and waiting is usually fine.

If the membrane covers most of the vaginal opening, and particularly if it is blocking urine flow, then it may be a good idea to see your doctor and get it treated. Simple local oestrogen cream will fix it after a few weeks, and you can then apply a barrier or nappy cream afterwards to help stop new adhesions developing.

TESTICLES

All newborn boys are checked to ensure that their testicles are 'down', but dads sometimes worry when they see that the future of their male ancestral lineage has been entrusted to someone whose scrotum seems empty. A flat, wrinkled little sack like a John Fowles' novel – a few surface layers but, underneath, no content.

Worry not. Remember your own pre-pubescent balls? I used to play hide-and-seek with mine, one disappearing while the other went on a fruitless search (told you I was a weird child). This is all possible courtesy of the cremaster muscle. Pre-puberty, this muscle can pull the testicles back up into the groin, leaving the scrotum empty. It's more common when it is cold, so the concerned dad might get some reassurance at bathtime – warmth and relaxation brings the testicles back down and there they can be seen and (gently) felt, nestled happily, if temporarily, in their rightful place.

PENISES

Why does that plural look odd to me? Penises. Maybe we don't often consider them in multiples, one being more than most of us can handle … anyhow, back to the point. Quite a few dads have quietly asked, of their healthy, chubby little baby, 'Is he alright, Doc? Down there, I mean, in the boy department? It just looks, well, a bit small.' And indeed, there lies little Gareth in all his naked, gurgling splendour, displaying not so much a chipolata as a baby earthworm with a severe case of social phobia.

Usually in these cases the main body of the penis is hidden by the chubbiness around the groin. Dad's anxiety can be assuaged by pressing on either side of Gareth's little organ, and bingo! The worm loses its shyness and appears in all its splendour.

FORESKINS

Leave it alone, dad (and mum). The foreskin is fixed to the head of the penis by adhesions and does not retract. These adhesions slowly break down over the years, but sometimes the foreskin does not fully retract until after puberty. So how to clean under it, I hear the cry again and again? You don't, and you don't need to. Wait until it is fully retractile, and then show him how – by which time he'll say, 'For God's sake …'

To circumcise or not to circumcise, as Hamlet meant to ask. Ha, and you thought dummies were controversial! The debate rages, mostly by parties who have a vested interest one way or the other. My (disinterested*) answer is simple – any minor health benefit from circumcision is offset by the minor risks, and so there is no strong medical reason to do it. Circumcise for religious reasons if you must, but not for health or hygiene, and certainly not because you want him to look like dad.

MY DAD iZ THE Best

---

* No, I'm not bored by the controversy, I mean disinterested as in its true meaning of unbiased.

CHAPTER 10

EXPECT THE UNEXPECTED

He'd just had his bath, he was clean and he smelt delicious. I lay on the bed and he lay on my tummy, his head rested on my chest. He was naked. I stroked his soft skin. To my horror, I felt my erection begin to grow. He was two weeks old.

That was an experience I had with my first child. I was appalled, surprised, disgusted, confused. Why was I reacting, apparently sexually, to this infant? Why was my penis, so often unpredictable in the past, choosing *this* moment to respond in this most unexpected and unwelcome manner? For God's sake, what did it think I was going to *do*?

On reflection, I realised that perhaps my body's unbidden and unwelcome reaction was not so surprising. For most adult men nearly all physical contact, especially skin-to-skin, is of a sexual nature – this was certainly true for myself. For 15 years or more, the only times I'd had skin touching my own was as a prelude to, or part of, sexual activity. As a fumbling teenager in the back of a friend's car, I'll never forget the first time I was allowed to tremblingly explore the forbidden secrets so temptingly concealed by the briefest of skirts – my hand on her thigh, skin so soft, so sensuous! This was a potent and memorable experience, and one that was reinforced many times in the following years. The connection between skin contact and sexual arousal became powerfully entrenched.

Your child was born with no clothes on and if he's anything like my kids he'll enjoy spending as much time as possible in the same state. Some of this time he'll spend climbing all over you, and some of this time you might be unclothed yourself. Even when you're both fully clothed, kids tend to treat their dads as human climbing frames, the main object seeming to be to tread on as many body parts as possible. The end result of all this is a degree of physical contact that most of us haven't, in recent years anyway, had with anyone other than a sexual partner.

Aside from sex, most of us men are not a very tactile lot; a firm handshake is the closest we come to physical intimacy.

Perhaps in this context it is less surprising that, in a moment of parental intimacy, with the combination of soft baby delicacy and my unbridled adoration of my new son, my body's instinctive responses were aroused.

I found at least a morsel of solace from this thought as I tried to understand what was happening. And I would discover that what was happening would recur on an occasional and unpredictable basis for several weeks to come.

THE UNSUSPECTING FATHER

Talking to other fathers, I know I'm not alone in having experienced this response. They too have been astonished by unexpected tumescence. Most have been confused, some appalled. I also suspect that there are dads out there who have been so guiltily shocked that they have subsequently avoided intimate contact with their child.

What is important is that the new father is made aware of this possible response and that you know that you're not the only one. Knowing that you may experience some kind of apparently erotic response to your own child might seem disgusting at first. Guilt and sex are familiar bedfellows, and seeing myself having a 'sexual' response to my own child certainly caused some initial guilt. The critical step was to realise that it did, in fact, have nothing to do with sex, and everything to do with a simple learned response. Physical yes, but not sexual. And over time, as my body 'learned' that this contact was different, non-sexual, the response faded and disappeared. Interestingly and perhaps predictably, it never happened with the next two babies.

DANGER!

Don't mistake your body's reaction (erection) for the sort of conscious, lustful, reciprocated desire that is familiar from adult relationships. It is essential to understand that, although the end result, the erection, is the same, the processes which lead to it are not.

Should you find yourself with the same experience, take no notice of your body's unbidden behaviour. Feel free to give the unruly member a stiff telling off and send it packing, then get on with enjoying your time with your baby. If you teach your body that this skin contact is different, a totally non-sexual pleasure, and ignore any penile response, then it will cease responding. Phew.

WHAT THE EXPERTS SAY

One of the reasons I feel this is an important topic is that, as far as I can tell, it has not been written about before. The only published work that I could find that comes close refers to a father's response in these terms:

> *Anti-touch and anti-sexual societies have spawned fathers who panic if they happen to experience sexual arousal with their child squirming on their lap, and*

*essentially punish the child severely by withdrawing
physical affection from his daughter or son. Or worse
still, is the father who acts on his sexual arousal using
the child as the defenseless object.*[11]

Although this is not about babies specifically, it addresses the two
concerns I mention above – rejection and abuse.

I have spoken to a number of experts – paediatricians, child
psychiatrists, psychoanalysts – all of whom agreed that the
possibility of a man experiencing a 'sexual' response to his baby
was a critical area for open discussion. As one put it, 'I suspect
that a normal father's erotic response to his own baby is one of
the last true taboos.'

CHAPTER 11

FOUR TRAPS WITH OLDER KIDS, AND HOW TO AVOID THEM

I CAN'T WAIT ...

I was 'caught' saying this with our first child: 'I can't wait until he starts walking'. He was probably six or seven months old at the time. The woman who heard me say this, a veteran of five kids, just said calmly:

'I used to say that with the first two or three. Then I realised I was always so preoccupied with looking forward to the next stage that I wasn't enjoying where they were at, at the time. It doesn't last long, you know, so appreciate what's happening now. He'll get to the next stage soon enough.'

It was good advice. It's easy to fall into the trap of eagerly anticipating the next stage: the first smile, the first words, being able to walk, to kick a ball (how many dads have I heard say, 'It'll be much more fun once we can play footy together'?). Yes, it will be fun – but so is now. Tiny babies are amazing, and they're only tiny for such a short time. Soak up every moment. The gummy smiles are unique, and once that first tooth comes through, they're gone forever.

I'll only say this once, then I promise never to repeat it (because you'll hear it again and again), but it's true – they grow up so fast. Enjoy every bit of what's happening now, because blink and it is over.

(OVER)PROTECTION

Attentive viewers of the wonderful Pixar movie *Finding Nemo* may remember an exchange between Marlin (daddy fish) and his ditzy acquaintance Dory. They're talking about Marlin's son, Nemo, who has gone missing:

Marlin: *'I promised I wouldn't let anything happen to him.'*

Dory: *'That's a funny thing to say.'*

Marlin: *'Why?'*

Dory: *'Because if nothing ever happens to him, nothing will ever happen to him.'*

Simple. Genius. A lovely reminder that there's a balance between sensible parental care and overprotection. No-one can tell you what the right balance is for you and your family, but it's a timely reminder that kids need the space and freedom to explore the world, take risks, make mistakes and learn from the consequences. I'm not suggesting you open the front door and usher them out to have a frolic on the freeway, just to remember that while cotton wool can cushion, it can also suffocate (pardon the somewhat tortuous metaphor).

In fact, *Finding Nemo* is pretty good reference material about being a father generally. If you haven't seen it, go and get a copy. If you have, watch it again.

'OH, ALRIGHT THEN ...'

You will know the concept of behaviour and reward; that by receiving something positive in response to 'it', we're more likely to do 'it' again, whatever 'it' is. A simple example of this is that you can teach a rat to press a lever by giving it food for doing so.

What is less well-known is that the behaviour change is also dependent on whether the reward is regular or irregular. Irregular, or inconsistent, reward can produce behaviour that is much harder to change than regular reward.

To illustrate, let's go back to our poor beleaguered rats, eagerly pressing their levers. If they've had food for every lever press, then the food stops, they press a few more times, then soon give up – you can almost hear them thinking, 'Stupid scientists, can't even get the food supply right'. Now, if they've been rewarded with food intermittently, so that they only get the food sometimes when the lever is pressed, and the food stops, those rats will keep pressing the lever much, much longer – 'There's still some there, there must be, just one more press ...' Think of the pokies, where sometimes the money comes out – 'Just one more press ...'

What has this to do with parenting? Only that it is how most parents end up dealing with their child's less desirable behaviours. Let's say the child is whining for a biscuit. Sometimes we hold firm with 'No', but at other times the whining gets the better of us and we've had enough and we utter the fateful words, 'Oh, alright then' – often followed by, 'Just this once'. (Ha!) Unwittingly we have just helped entrench that behaviour even more strongly.[12] Which leads us to ...

CONSISTENCY

So, it's simple, huh? No means no and keep it that way. Well yes – and no. While consistency is important, that does not mean that decisions can't be changed. The consistency has to be in who is in charge of the decisions.

Let's take the Great Biscuit Conundrum we touched on above. Responding to the whining with, 'Oh, alright then' is intermittent reward, designed to entrench whining as a behaviour. But, let's imagine we've said 'No', but then think, 'Mmm, it's an hour until dinner, I'm all out of carrot sticks and fresh fruit, she hasn't eaten for four hours – perhaps a biscuit is not so unreasonable'. What to do? My answer is that we resolutely say 'No' to the whining and then, when all protest has ceased and a decent interval has occurred, we say something like, 'You know what, Schmookums, daddy has changed his mind. You've been very good, and it's still a while until dinner, so let's have a biscuit'. In this version, Schmookums has been rewarded not for her whining but for her good behaviour. Despite her appalling pet name.

Which leads us to …

'JUST SAY YES'

Simon Carr (no relation, sadly, even though he too is English) wrote a wonderful book[13] about being a single dad bringing up boys. One of his principles was that, pretty much whatever the request, he would 'Just say Yes', and he writes of a joyous and sometimes bewildering chaos that ensued. I'm not sure I'd go quite that far, but I rather like the concept – one of the things modern parents tend to do is have 'No' as the first response (see '(Over)Protection'):

- Can we play in the puddles?
- No, you'll ruin your shoes.
- Can I wear my Batman suit?
- No, you'll be too hot.
- Can we put the cat in the dryer?
- No, it'll leave fur on the washing.

OK, so let's not substitute a 'Yes' for every 'No'. But if for you or your partner the knee-jerk response tends to be negative, try pausing and having a go at something more positive:

- Can we bring all the cushions in and make a cubby?
- Yes

- Can we make a bow and arrow?
- Yes

It's not a bad habit to develop, particularly as the kid(s) get older:

- Dad, can I get my tongue pierced?
- Yes

Just remember the balance …

- But not until you've finished primary school.

AND THAT'S OUR YOUNGEST, TOMMY, WHO WE USE TO STOP THE TABLE WOBBLING...

POSTSCRIPT

This was a long time ago for me. At the time of writing, I have two kids at university and one at high school. Before writing that last sentence, I made brunch for my son and his girlfriend. It seems almost impossible to connect the strapping great 6 foot 2 inch* young man who just hoovered through bacon, eggs, mushrooms, tomatoes, toast and juice with the tiny baby I held in my arms with such awe 22 years ago. He was, as my mother the psychologist put it so nicely in her clipped English, 'a *very* difficult little boy'. Bursting with energy and irritability, he was described by his Prep teacher, after his first day at primary school, as 'like a little volcano'. He was a boy who needed a lot of his dad, who needed a bucket of maleness in his life. Fortunately for him, I adored him. Still do. I was more than happy to roll my sleeves up and get stuck in. Stopping work – 'outside the home' – one day a week was the best decision I ever made, even though the financial compromise meant keeping the same Commodore for 17 years (and still going). It helped make sure there was enough time, that the bucket was full enough.

His sister was born 18 months after him. I'll never forget walking around the labour ward with her in my arms, tears in my eyes as I

---

* I'm 6 foot 3 – one of the few areas where I still reign supreme!

muttered, 'I've got a daughter, I've got a daughter' over and over again. (Now that I commit this to print, it sounds pretty wet. But it's true. Anyhow, no-one reads these bits at the end of a book. Do they?) Two kids, boy and girl. I was hit by a shocking realisation, something I hadn't seen coming. I was now officially a grown-up.

One of each. Such an unbelievable privilege. Each of them so different, yet so much fun. Such a wonderful start to life as a parent. Rose-tinted retrospectacles? Perhaps. Yes, there were times when I would happily have chucked one or the other out of the window, times when I hated the job, hated them (see p. 36). But these were brief moments, the occasional discord in an otherwise magical symphony, the odd unforced error in a near-perfect game, a few scattered portraits interloping in an exhibition of abstract expressionism. They were uncommon enough to inspire excruciating metaphor.

Then the third baby question. She wanted one more, I didn't. Me all practical and logical – we have one of each, they're healthy, we're happy, we can afford them, they fit in our car, what is it that you don't have enough of that you want more of? Relentless, logical and so right. She had, of course, no answer. Which proved how right I was.

Naturally, then, the third baby came along. As so often, it was my Mum (psychologist, remember?) who made me see sense: 'It's not about logic, it's just a feeling. She's a woman, she wants another baby. It's biology.' Ah. The old logic vs. feelings battle. See Chapter 3, Venus and Mars.

Fortunately, third baby was not only healthy, but an absolute delight. 'As fit as a trout', the obstetrician announced somewhat perplexingly. I didn't ever want her to hear second-hand about my reluctance to go beyond two kids, so as soon as she was verbal enough to understand, I explained it to her. Her version? 'Daddy didn't want a third baby. Then he got me.' It takes a four-year-old to reduce a 12-month battle between adults to its essence.

Was all that time and energy invested in being a nurturing father worth it? I suspect you know the answer. The proof for me is that I have a relationship with my adult children that I would never have dared hope for. We do stuff together – travel, play sport, go camping, watch movies, cook and wash-up, play Scrabble (still). We talk. And yes, it did actually happen. First daughter was three or four years old, she was on the toilet, my wife and I were both at home, and the cry came, 'Daaaad!'

As I went to the rescue, you can imagine how proud I felt.

REFERENCES

[1] Bowlby, J 1951, 'Maternal care and mental health', *Bulletin of the World Health Organization*, vol. 3, no. 3, p. 363.

[2] Mead, M 1949, 'Human fatherhood is a social invention', in *Male and female: A study of the sexes in a changing world*, p. 192, William Morrow and Company, New York.

[3] McCain, MN & Fraser Mustard, J 1999, *Reversing the real brain drain – Early years study: Final report*, Ontario Children's Secretariat, Toronto, Canada.

[4] Russell, G et al. 1999, *Fitting fathers into families: Men and the fatherhood role in contemporary Australia*. Department of Family and Community Services, Canberra.

[5] Odent, M 2008, 'A top obstetrician on why men should never be at the birth of their child', Mail Online, viewed 13 March 2012, <www.dailymail.co.uk/femail/article-559913/A-obstetrician-men-NEVER-birth-child.html>.

[6] National Sexual Assault, Domestic Family Violence Counselling Service, 24 hours: 1800 RESPECT or 1800 737 732, 24 hour online counselling service: <www.1800respect.org.au.>; Relationships Australia, Support groups and counselling on relationships, and for abusive and abused partners: 1300 364 277, < www.relationships.com.au>.

[7] ABC, George Negus Tonight 2004, Co-sleeping and Dr Nick Carr interview, viewed 13 March 2012, <www.abc.net.au/gnt/future/Transcripts/s1058920.htm>.

[8] McKenna, JJ & Gettler, LT 2008, 'Cultural influences on infant and childhood sleep biology and the science that studies it: Toward a more inclusive paradigm II', in C Marcus, J Carroll, D Donnelly & G Loughlin, (eds), *Sleep and breathing in children: Developmental changes in sleep patterns*, 2nd ed., pp. 183–221, Informa Healthcare USA, New York.

University of Notre Dame, Mother–Baby Behavioral Sleep Laboratory 2012, 'Safe cosleeping guidelines', viewed 14 March 2012, <http://cosleeping.nd.edu/safe-co-sleeping-guidelines>.

[9] Jordan, B, Heine, RG, Meehan, M, Catto-Smith, AG & Lubitz, L 2006, 'Effect of antireflux medication, placebo and infant mental health intervention on persistent crying: A randomised clinical trial', *Journal of Paediatrics and Child Health*, Jan-Feb; vol. 42, nos 1–2, pp. 49–58.

[10] RSPCA 2011, Will my new-born baby be safe around my dog?, viewed 13 March 2012, <kb.rspca.org.au/Will-my-new-born-baby-be-safe-around-my-dog_17.html>.

[11] Hatfield, RW 1994, 'Touch and human sexuality', in V. Bullough, B. Bullough, & A. Stein (eds), *Human sexuality: An encyclopedia*, Garland Publishing, New York.

[12] Carr, N & Carr, J 1999, 'Reinforcement schedules and the management of childhood behaviours', *Behavioural and Cognitive Psychotherapy*, vol. 27, pp. 89–96.

[13] Carr, S 2000, *The boys are back in town*, Arrow, UK.

FURTHER READING

The dad factor: How father–baby bonding helps a child for life, Richard Fletcher, Finch, Sydney, NSW, 2011.

An excellent Australian book that discusses in more detail the importance of fathers, including the supporting scientific evidence.

First-time father: Pregnancy, birth and starting out as a dad, Tony White and Dr Graeme Russell, Finch, Sydney, NSW, 2005.

Another lovely Australian book, and is co-authored by a GP, so perhaps I'm biased. Includes many anecdotes from new fathers.

BIKER DAD

ABOUT BEING A GREAT DAD

My dad's got mojo, Gary Bertwistle, Wrightbooks, Milton, Qld, 2010.

Chatty, easy to read and with some nice tips about being a great dad – if you can get past all the 'When I was keynote speaker at an incredibly important conference ...' intros.

A man's guide to raising kids, Michael Grose, Random House, North Sydney, NSW, 2000.

Smart stuff from a man who really knows.

Being a great dad for dummies, Stefan Korn, Scott Lancaster and Eric Mooij, Wiley, Milton, Qld, 2010.

Sounds appalling, but isn't.

SERIOUS STUFF

The magic years, Selma Fraiberg, Methuen, London, 1959.

Seminal text from one of the pioneers of infant mental health.

A good enough parent: A book on child rearing, Bruno Bettelheim, Knopf, NY, 1987.

A timely reminder, in our search for parenting perfectionism, that kids are resilient. We don't get it right all the time, but we can still be good enough, and that's OK.